THE BATTLE FOR BERLIN

THE BATTLE
FOR BERLIN

John Strawson

Whoever controls Berlin will rule Germany;
whoever controls Germany rules Europe

LENIN

Charles Scribner's Sons
New York

© John Strawson 1974

Library of Congress Catalogue No 73-19092
ISBN 0-684-13808-5

Printed in Great Britain

CONTENTS

ACKNOWLEDGMENTS

Writing a book about Berlin has held a particular interest for me because from 1970–72 I was a member of the quadripartite military staff charged with making plans to counter attempts by the Soviet Union or the German Democratic Republic to interrupt Allied access to and from the city. My duties carried me often to Berlin itself, and also to the capitals of those four countries concerned with such planning, Paris, Bonn, Washington and London. The consequences of the battle for Berlin, together with the problems of access to it across the GDR, were thus my daily fare for two years. The city itself has left an indelible impression of its ability to survive all sieges. Nor can I forget my first visit there – at the time of the British military tattoo in 1947, when my regiment, the 4th Hussars, took part and enacted a fox hunting scene. Berlin was still ruined, grey and beggarly, yet the Berliners' response to a display of military bands, horses, drill and other spectacles was astonishing in its volume and enthusiasm. It helped me to understand what I later read of their behaviour during the years of Allied bombing and the dreadful destruction caused by the final battle for Berlin.

I would like once again to thank Mr Peter Kemmis Betty for his advice in the planning of this book and for his suggestions about improving the first draft. My thanks are due to the following authors and publishers for permission to quote from the books named: Sir Isaiah Berlin, *Mr Churchill in 1940*, John Murray for pages 45n and 52; Richard Brett-Smith, *Berlin '45; the grey city*, Macmillan for pages 7, 115–16 and 159–60; Vasili I. Chuikov, *The End of the Third Reich*, Macgibbon & Kee for pages 123–5 and 126–8; Winston Churchill, *The Second World War*, Cassell & Co Ltd for pages 15, 16, 60, 152 and 160; Alan Clark, *Barbarossa*, Hutchinson & Co Ltd for page 75; General Heinz Guderian, *Panzer Leader*, Michael Joseph for pages 36, 43, 78 and 80; Ursula von Kardorff, *Diary of a Nightmare, Berlin 1942–45*, Rupert Hart-Davis for page 68; Erich Kuby, *The Russians and Berlin 1945*, William Heinemann Ltd for pages 99–101 and 153–5; B. H. Liddell Hart, *The Tanks, Vol II*, Collins for pages 91–2 and 157–8; Sir Martin Lindsay, *So Few Got Through*, Cassell & Co Ltd for pages 89–90 and 98–9; Alexander McKee,

Acknowledgments

The Race for the Rhine Bridges, Souvenir Press for page 96; General Shtemenko, Article in *Military History Journal* for pages 69–70; Konstantin Simonov, *Aus den Kriegstagebüchern,* Neue Welt for pages 125–6; Albert Speer, *Inside the Third Reich,* Weidenfeld & Nicolson for pages 19, 23, 24, 67, 121–2, 134n and 137; H. G. von Studnitz, *While Berlin Burns,* Weidenfeld & Nicolson for pages 67–8; The Times Publishing Company, *The Times Literary Supplement* for pages 58 and 161; John Toland, *The Last 100 Days,* Arthur Barker Ltd for pages 122–3; H. R. Trevor Roper, *The Last Days of Hitler,* Macmillan for pages 61–2, 133, 136 and 142; Pavel Troyanovsky, *The Last Days of Berlin,* Soviet News London for pages 152–3; General Helmuth Weidling, *Der Endkampf in Berlin,* Wehrwissenschaftliche Rundschau for page 150; General W. Wenck, *Berlin's Last 10 Days,* Stern Magazine, Hamburg for pages 131, 141 and 148; Chester Wilmot, *The Struggle for Europe,* Collins for pages 24, 35 and 112; Georgi K. Zhukov, *Marshal Zhukov's Greatest Battles,* Macdonald for pages 10 and 155–6.

I am grateful to the Editors of *The Army Quarterly and Defence Journal* for permission to make use of material which appeared in articles under the title of *Macaulay as Military Historian* in 1963 and 1964. For all their help in getting books of reference for me, I wish to thank Mr John E. Garrod, Librarian of the SHAPE Military Library and his assistants, Mr D. W. King of the Ministry of Defence Library and his staff, Mr K. M. White of the Staff College, Camberley and his staff. My particular thanks are due to Corporal D. Parry, RAF for typing the book's first draft and to Mrs E. M. Garton for typing and re-typing subsequent drafts and also for helping me with proof reading and the Index. As always, my wife gave me the most valuable advice throughout the production of this book.

Finally, author and publishers wish to thank the Imperial War Museum for permission to reproduce the photographs appearing in this book.

ILLUSTRATIONS

PROLOGUE

History is the science of what never happens twice.
                                                    VALÉRY

Was Valéry right? Or can it be argued that when thinking of military
affairs, history is rather the science of what seems to happen again and
again? If we wished to generalize about British military history, we
might say that it falls broadly into two categories – one part a series of
bold ventures, like Clive's seizure of Arcot or Wolfe's capture of
Quebec, infinite in their vision, astonishing in their almost insolent
disregard for the military odds, incalculable in their political repercussions, and responsible for writing page after page of military glory
constantly read and re-read to this day; the other part a weary, stale,
flat and unprofitable catalogue of indecisive, ill-judged and ponderous
campaigns, lightened only by perseverance and redeemed only by
virtue of possessing powerful allies. So sharp a distinction makes it easy
to separate the wars of Empire from the struggles for Europe. In the
first, innovation, freedom of action, boldness of execution and *gain*
were all to hand. In the second the tables were exactly turned – loss
was grievous, enterprise sick, manoeuvre shackled, initiative stifled.
And the main circumstance which conditioned these latter operations
was almost always the same – heavy odds against this country, a condition which in turn meant that there was no alternative to a long
haul.

No matter whether we are thinking of Philip v, Louis xiv, Napoleon,
Imperial Germany or Hitler, a combination of strategic audacity and
tactical professionalism on our enemies' part never quite managed to
do the trick, to bring off the one coup which would put the game in the
bag, give blitzkrieg a proper conclusion – the subjugation of England.
It has sometimes been supposed that the defeat of the Spanish Armada

suddenly and decisively made all the difference between the positions of England and Spain and resulted in the rise of the former and decline of the latter. Professor Garrett Mattingly has, of course, properly disposed of such rubbishy over-simplifications. Like Dunkirk, the affair of 1588 was for this country a mere evasion of defeat, an episode in a long dragged out war. Yet the plan itself – Philip's coordination of the ideas of his ablest seaman, Santa Cruz, to launch a great expedition of over 500 sail from Spain, and of his ablest soldier, Parma, to nip across the channel in barges one night with an army of some 35,000 foot and horse – was bold indeed. The great Enterprise naturally depended on there being no mistakes, on nothing going wrong. Its very rigidity and complexity were its undoing rather than its lack of strategic soundness. Had Parma and Medina Sidonia done what Philip told them to do, it is difficult to see how Elizabeth and Leicester could have prevented a landing. How the English trained bands would have fared against the Spanish infantry is as much a matter for conjecture as whether the Militia could have taken on the Grande Armée or the Home Guard the Wehrmacht. But as we know, however bold, the best laid schemes of men can go awry.

Napoleon described himself as the boldest general who ever lived. Yet he did not dare embark on the invasion of England. It was not for want of making plans. After the Treaty of Tilsit, with Russia in his alliance and the rest of Europe more or less compliant, the Emperor reverted to his former intentions. The entire maritime forces of the Continent, 250 sail of the line, would be mustered, and thus supported he would lead a European army to London. Half his fleet would be employed against England's colonies and entice away much of the British navy. The other half would escort Napoleon's great flotilla across the Channel. Such was the Emperor's plan. But it was never carried out. Dissipating the Grand Army in Spain was the course he chose instead. Once again England's defeat was avoided, but it was avoided not so much by English endeavour as by her enemies' errors.

Canning did well to refer to Pitt as the pilot that weathered the storm, for he certainly had a storm to weather. Macaulay is not kind about Pitt's aptitude for the conduct of war. 'His military administration was that of a driveller.' He reminds us that Pitt simply misunderstood the nature of the war in which he was engaged and therefore completely mismanaged it. In spite of the totality of the danger, in spite of having absolute command of unlimited resources, Pitt did not create large, well-equipped and successful armies. Instead he embarked upon one disastrous expedition after another and was saved only by the existence of the English Navy and his own eloquence in the House of Commons. After many years of war and countless expenditure of life and treasure, 'the English Army, under Pitt, was the laughing-stock of all Europe'.

It was left to Wellington to reverse this judgment, yet Wellington was not called the Fabian General for nothing. It is curious that Wellington owes much of his greatness not – as for example his co-architect of victory, Nelson, does – to an absolute determination to seek out and bring the enemy to bay, an all consuming spirit of the offensive which by indulgence in one pell-mell battle after another, would make England safe simply by virtue of having annihilated the opposition. In quite a different way, Wellington was determined to avoid, if possible, a great battle of any sort. His reasoning was clear. It was not that he misunderstood – what Hitler so clearly saw and delighted in – that the principal feature of war was violence. It was rather that violence for its own sake had no appeal to him. He would resort to it only for the attainment of a particular object. Thus he could know when to retreat and dare to do so a dozen times in order to preserve England's only Army. He simply was not prepared to risk it on one turn of pitch-and-toss. But when violence was indispensable, as for example at Ciudad Rodrigo or Badajos, he did not hesitate.

It was well said of the Earl of Essex – Cromwell's contemporary, not Elizabeth's – that his military errors were caused by political timidity. He could not see that it was impossible to impose his will on others with moderate military activity. Essex practised moderation in war because he was equally fearful of success or failure. He shunned vigour and decision as if he dreaded their effect on events – strange recipe for a commander. How differently Prince Rupert viewed military operations. To him violence, dash, quick decision were the very essence of war. Yet the results he achieved were equally indecisive. He was always darting here and there, charging furiously home, routing and scattering his enemies. He won a hundred skirmishes but not a single campaign. He could never resist the temptation of one more charge. On perhaps one occasion only was his strategic vision sound. If the King had taken his advice and pushed on to London in August 1643, he might have had no more fighting to do. Yet impetuosity by itself will not do. We need too patience, discipline and the ability to unite moderation and violence if we are to win battles and wars at the same moment. Concentration on one alone – always provided the enemy is not already beaten – will hardly do the trick. A single violent campaign like the battle of France in 1940 was successful only because blitzkrieg encountered the worst of all military dispositions – passive dispersion.

It was a coalition of violence and moderation which made England's colonial wars so uniquely successful. Plassey and Assaye, followed as they were by negotiation and concession, conquered a sub-continent. Copenhagen, complemented by Nelson's diplomacy, robbed Napoleon of another. But it was in each case the success of violence which opened the door to the further success of moderation. The reverse equation is less easy of achievement. Gladstone's moderation could no more prevent the violent death of Gordon than Chamberlain's could persuade Hitler that he could not have Poland too without a fight. For the British, audacity and perseverance were more often than not enough to win the day in distant places when the interference of Government was too late to influence events. But the progress of their arms in Europe was often put out of balance either by the procrastination of Government, the indifference of commanders in the field or their slavish adherence to the rules of the day. Macaulay made it clear that 'a quick eye, a cool head and a stout heart will do more to make a general than all the diagrams of Jomini,' Yet more often than not the diagrams of Jomini have wielded such a fascination for generals that time and again they have led them to failure.

Churchill reiterated the point plainly enough in the biography of his great ancestor when he argued that the success of a commander does not arise from following rules or models. 'There is no surer road to disaster than to imitate the plans of bygone heroes and fit them to novel situations.' The War of the Spanish Succession presents us with a notable illustration in the way that Lord Galway conducted himself. That Galway was an experienced commander no one would deny. That he was familiar with campaigning conditions in Spain was equally recognized. And that his failure in 1707 was as a result of his insistence that war was an exact science from which all original ideas should be excluded was made equally clear in that, having embarked on the battle of Almanza in a manner with which the text books could have found no fault, it took him only a few hours to lose the best part of twenty thousand men, all his guns and baggage, over a hundred colours, the campaign itself and almost the whole of Spain. How different a man was one of his contemporaries – Charles Mordaunt, Earl of Peterborough. He possessed the very qualities most appropriate to the peculiar demands of the campaign in which he was engaged. He was able to do much with extremely slender resources. Audacity and novelty were second nature to him. He knew when to strike a decisive blow, how to do so and above all, how to exploit its success. Having embarked upon a course of action, nothing could deflect him. He was dismayed neither by unfavourable odds nor by the inconstancy of the elements. His energy overcame difficulties which would have caused other men to falter. But it was his irresistible capriciousness which robbed him of the confidence of his employers.

If we had to find a modern Galway and a modern Peterborough, we would discover an endless catalogue of the former and a depressing dearth of the latter. Galways were two a penny among the very nation which should have bred the Peterboroughs – France. It has been said of the French military leaders that between 1918 and 1940 they had learned nothing and forgotten everything. So that Gamelin was as incapable of understanding what was happening at Sedan in May 1940 as he was incapable of checking the German break-through there, and if we leave de Gaulle aside for the moment, most of the French generals looked on the 1940 battle through the eyes of Gamelin.

It would be equally useless to search for a Peterborough in the ranks of British generals of 1940. It is true that for learning and courtesy, for steady courage, for the fertility and activity of his mind, for generosity and humanity, we might need to look no further than a Wavell or an Alexander. But where was the wit which filled dispatches with epigrams, the eccentricities which turned the rules of the game upside down, the novelty, the sheer love of excitement? Nor do we find all this among the Germans even though, for novelty and audacity, men like Guderian and Rommel could hardly be bettered. Indeed the whole idea of blitzkrieg was to demoralize and paralyse the enemy by a combination of surprise, speed, unanticipated violence and momentum. A gigantic all-devouring blow – this was what blitzkrieg meant. Yet the lesson was completely wasted on Germany's enemies.

Indeed one of the most remarkable features of the Second World War was that although Hitler demonstrated time and again that blitzkrieg was a campaign winner, none of the armies opposing him ever had either the audacity or the expertise to give him a taste of his own medicine. The armies subjected to blitzkrieg were totally ill-equipped to cope with such a method of making war. They did not understand it. The Poles chose to string their inadequate army out on their western border in dispositions best designed to induce instant collapse. They did not lack courage. They were simply overwhelmed. The French presented Hitler with the glittering temptation of a weak centre and that, combined with paralysis of command and will, was enough to destroy them. The British in the desert were confounded by Rommel. If the business of successfully resisting attack in war may be summed up as having the elasticity to recoil without disintegration, it implies also that you must, in addition to avoiding defeat, be able to inflict it. England's case was special as the British Army was able to recoil across the Channel. But 'wars are not won by evacuations' and England's army was puny. Despite gallant successes in East and North Africa, this fact alone meant that England could not fight without allies and in nearly all the wars England fought against a European tyranny, allies were usually both hard to find and expensive. That Hitler should have made a gift to England of two allies, and those two the most powerful nations in the world uncommitted to war, must always rate as one of the most crass ineptitudes of strategy that will ever be perpetrated. Yet even then these three allies did not indulge in blitzkrieg. They had neither the psychological makeup, the military expertise, either in generalship or low level tactics, nor the capacity for gambling that were the indispensable ingredients of such campaigns as those the Germans conducted in Poland, France and Russia. But would blitzkrieg have worked against the Germans? It may be doubted. Even if Montgomery had been allowed to launch a great offensive on a single narrow front – as he so greatly desired and so often urged Eisenhower to allow him to do – it is as certain as anything is in war that he would have failed, for just as men like von Rundstedt, Guderian and von Manteuffel understood how to initiate blitzkrieg, so they understood the antidote – the rapid sealing off of the dangerous penetration by mixed teams of artillery, tanks, engineers and panzer grenadiers. The truth was that, although the Germans had time and time again 'bounced' an enemy, they were exceptionally difficult foes to bounce in return.

Thus, unlike the blitzkrieg campaigns which lasted a few weeks, it took the British (assisted latterly by the Americans) two years to turn the Germans out of North Africa; it took the Allies two years to advance from there to the Alps; it took the Russians four years to defeat Barbarossa; and – after three years of this latter campaign which knocked the stuffing out of the Wehrmacht – it took the Americans, British and French another year to advance from Normandy to the Elbe. Given Hitler's predictable refusal to surrender or compromise, therefore, the battle for Berlin was bound to be a long drawn out affair.

I

À BERLIN

Twelve months ago the armoured cars began to carry the
chalked inscription à Berlin *which pretty French and Belgian*
girls scrawled on their plating . . .

RICHARD BRETT-SMITH

It might be argued that the whole of the war against Nazi Germany
was one great battle for Berlin for it was only the fall of that city, or
rather the fall of one man besieged there, which brought it all to an
end. The battle lasted an unconscionable time, and when the Western
Allies or the Soviet Union defined military objectives, they repeatedly
nominated Berlin as the goal of their armies. They were more circum-
spect as to how it was to be taken, and in any case such definition of an
objective made little sense in terms of realizing it until the city was
within reach of their armies. But when was this and what is meant by
within reach?

Once the Wehrmacht had finally reconciled itself to a strategy of
defence, in the East defence on the Vistula and in the West defence on
the Rhine, once Germany itself was about to be properly invaded, in
other words from January 1945 onwards, the battle for Berlin – then
but a few hundred miles distant from each main enemy force – had
begun. It is not our purpose here to trace the operations of every corps
or division, whether Russian, German, British or American, engaged in
the last four or five months of the war. Rather it is to give impressions
– impressions of the respective Allied strategies which determined the
course of the war at this stage and of the Germans', or more properly
the Führer's, attempts to prolong the war beyond the point of its
having been lost, impressions of what some of the fighting was actually
like and of what influence the great leaders of both sides exerted upon
the whole affair. Nor would the story be complete without reminding
ourselves that the city's position today shows us that the battle for
Berlin is not and perhaps never will be over.

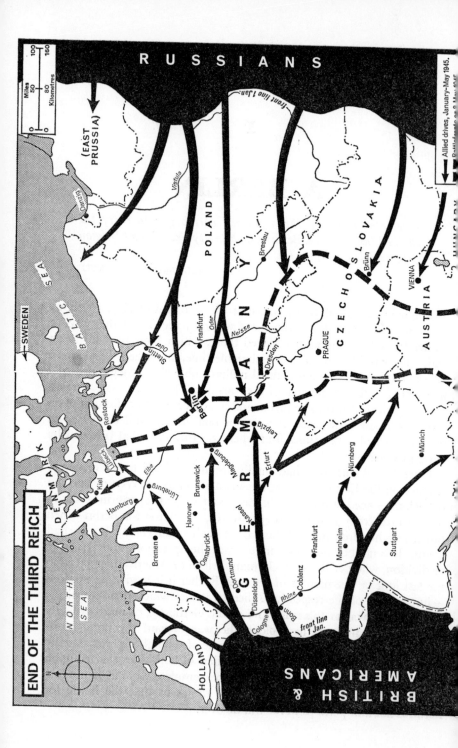

END OF THE THIRD REICH

It is fitting at the very outset to have a picture of the principal operations which led to Berlin's capture, that is to consider very roughly what happened on the Eastern and Western fronts. It might be supposed that only the Eastern front matters because it was the Red Army which took Berlin. Yet in spite of all the Western Allies' dithering and Eisenhower's declared intention not to go for the city, he toyed with the idea of its capture, and in this he was strongly pressed by the British, right up to the last moment. In any event only the interplay of the two fronts, east and west, explains the whole strategic circumstance which allowed the Red Army to take Berlin at all as early as it did.

On the Eastern front planning for the final battle of the war began in the Soviet High Command in October 1944. The plan was for an advance from the Vistula to Berlin and beyond – the entire operation to take only about six weeks – two to reach the Bydgoszcz-Poznan-Breslau-Vienna line and another month to eliminate the German forces and take Berlin. The date of the offensive was to be 20 January 1945 and it was subsequently brought forward by eight days. Three Army Groups or *fronts* would take part – 1st and 2nd Belorussian commanded respectively by Zhukov and Rokossovsky, and 1st Ukrainian under Konev. Between them they had two and a half million men against less than a million Germans, while their superiority in material resources averaged some three or four to one. What happened? The first part of the programme went roughly according to plan and by the beginning of February the Red Army was on the general line Königsberg-Küstrin-Breslau, that is on the River Oder opposite Berlin and a mere 40 miles from the city. But then there was a pause and the second part of the plan did not get under way until mid-April. When it did, Berlin was quickly surrounded and taken by Zhukov's and Konev's Army Groups while the Russians also advanced to the Elbe-Mulde line, agreed meeting point with Eisenhower's forces.

It was Stalin who decided not to press on after the initial and substantial success. Why? Was it fear of German counter-attacks from the north, or determination with Berlin virtually in the bag to get his hands on as much of south-eastern Europe as he could too, or what? The conundrum is made still more perplexing by recalling that *after* agreement with the Allies as to where their respective armies should meet (well to the west of the city) Stalin asked his principal subordinates: 'Who is to capture Berlin, we or the Allies?' and thus appeared to be turning the Red Army's final operations into a race for the capital. Zhukov maintained that neither his own Army Group nor Konev's was in a position to move on Berlin in February 1945. Losses of men and equipment, supply difficulties, lack of advance air support, to say nothing of the enemy's capability to interfere, all dictated against it. General Chuikov, on the other hand, commanding 8th Guards Army under Zhukov, troops which eventually occupied the Chancellory, did not, as we shall see, agree and he claimed that the war could have been ended in February. He also recorded a meeting between Zhukov and his subordinate commanders on 4 February at which the advance on Berlin was being discussed. During the meeting Stalin telephoned Zhukov to ask what his plans were. When told that they were about to execute the Berlin operation, Stalin quickly told Zhukov to stop that and instead deal with the German forces of Army Group Vistula in Pomerania.

Because of this the actual thrust on Berlin did not start until 16 April. The plan was broadly that Zhukov's Army Group would go for and take the city while Konev's 1st Ukrainian *front* would advance from the Neisse river to cut off the German Army Group Centre from Berlin and so secure Zhukov's southern flank. Meanwhile Rokossovsky's 2nd Belorussian *front* was to move four days later to protect the northern flank. Zhukov's own estimate of the battle ahead of him was full of concern for its immense difficulty:

> The unusual and highly complex offensive against Berlin required the most careful preparation at all *front* and army levels. Troops of the 1st Belorussian *front* were expected to break through a deeply echeloned defence zone extending from the Oder River all the way to heavily fortified Berlin. Never before in the experience of warfare had we been called upon to capture a city as large and as heavily fortified as Berlin. Its total area was almost 350 square miles. Its subway and other widespread underground engineering networks provided ample possibilities for troop movements. The city itself and its suburbs had been carefully prepared for defence. Every street, every square, every alley, building, canal and bridge represented an element in the city's defence system.

In spite of all these difficulties by 20 April the artillery of 3rd Shock Army had opened fire on Berlin and next day the leading troops of this and two more armies, 2nd Guards Tank and 47th, broke into the outskirts of the city. The final phase of the battle for Berlin had started. It was to last for eleven more days. On 2 May General Weidling, Berlin commandant, surrendered and it was all over. These last battles between 16 April and the German capitulation cost the Red Army over

300,000 casualties, a huge sum. There could be no more eloquent testimony as to how hard a struggle it had been.

Throughout the battle Hitler was in the Bunker, resolved to stay in Berlin until the end, for he persuaded himself that as long as he remained there the city might not fall. In one sense he was right, since his own death preceded its capture or at least the capture of its last remnants. While he was still alive he continued to harbour his crazy notions of saving the Thousand Year Reich and its capital, of conducting one more great battle which would lead to the Red Army's greatest defeat. He stuck to his established practice of manipulating real armies* and when they had been dissipated or destroyed, marshalling phantom ones; he presided over meaningless military conferences, gave fictional orders, shuffled buttons on out of date maps, and as usual put down the cause of all failure to treachery, never to his own bankrupt and fatal conduct of war. Berlin survived but two days after Hitler's death, the Third Reich but a week. The great city he had designed with Albert Speer, a Berlin to dwarf Paris, was an illusion. The projected capital of a huge empire for the Master Race and its subjugated Slav dominions would never now be built. Instead a shattered shell would be looted and lounged in by Slav *Untermenschen* until what was left of the city was partially rescued by the Western Allies.

As for these same Western Allies, could they in fact have won a race for Berlin as Stalin had implied? They had done a good deal of talking and at various times had promised themselves the great prize. If action were to match all this talk, surely now, the beginning of 1945, was the time to get on with it, when the Wehrmacht was again shifting its weight to the East and simply making do in the West. Advantage had to be taken of the Germans' desperate plight – how to fight a successful war on two fronts with the initiative at neither. In short at the moment when Hitler's strategy gave them an opportunity which had never occurred before and would never recur, the Allies simply had to sink their differences and move forward united, concentrated and irresistible. It was an opportunity they elected to forgo. Instead old controversies were revived to unbalance and embitter Allied counsels. What was the right thing to do, they argued – to advance on a broad front as hitherto or to go for the single and narrow *Schwerpunkt* across the Rhine? Indeed, what were the objectives themselves to be?

Eisenhower, who was nothing if not consistent, wanted as usual to

*The German forces concerned were Army Group Vistula (Heinrici), 9th Army (Busse), 12th Army (Wenck) and Army Group Centre (Schörner). For deployment see Map on p. 147.

play it safe, to advance everywhere and be secure everywhere. He stuck to his broad front strategy. In the north Montgomery's group of armies was to drive across the Lower Rhine and into the North German Plain in order to exploit that area's great potential for mobile operations and to deny Germany use of the Ruhr. Bradley, further south, was to attack towards Kassel, complete the Ruhr's envelopment and drive on to link up with the Russians. That in broad outline was Eisenhower's plan. It was exactly this aim of advancing everywhere which stuck in the gullet of the British Chiefs of Staff. They simply did not believe that their forces were strong enough for both operations. They dreaded a rapid advance in the north by the Red Army who might then reach the North Sea before themselves. So, they argued, as so often before, that there should be only one main thrust, and that in the north. The British, who, in spite of all their adaptability, could be as single-minded as any, also took the astonishing step of reapplying their pressure to have one land battle commander-in-chief under Eisenhower. Had they had their way and had Montgomery been appointed to this position there was a strong likelihood that Bradley and Patton would have resigned as they had often threatened to do. But it was not Montgomery whom Churchill had in mind. He wanted Alexander. He was sure that Alexander would direct Allied land operations in accordance with his, Churchill's, views, in other words in pursuit of proper British political objectives. There was such a weight of American opposition to the whole idea that the British dropped it.

It must have come as something of a surprise to the British that the result of the Rhine battles (leaving aside what might have been done *after* crossing the Rhine) showed Eisenhower to be right both in his strategic plan and in his command arrangements. The fact was that by this time he was sure of himself. He had grasped once and for all that two of the old principles of war mouthed a thousand times by students of war the world over – concentration of force and balanced reserves – were sound. Break the rules and you usually went wrong. Stick to them and you very often won battles. Certainly the Supreme Commander had by this time received such personal confirmation of this point that he did not forget it. So successful were his operations during February and March that whereas at the time of Yalta the Allied armies in the West were stuck and the Red Army was everywhere sweeping forward, later, after crossing the Rhine in March, for Eisenhower the roads to Berlin and most of Germany were open, and in the East the Germans were holding firm on the Oder-Neisse line. Of course a switch of the German armies had contributed to this – from the Allied side – agreeable state of affairs. What is surprising is that this particular tide was not taken at the flood. After Model's armies were encircled in the Ruhr, a gap of 200 miles was made in the German Western defences, and Eisenhower had resources enough, both fighting and administrative, to motor to Berlin. Only other, non-military considerations could have stopped him.

There was no shortage of these other considerations, and one of them was the growing distrust of Soviet Russia felt by Roosevelt and Churchill. Churchill, while expecting Stalin to revoke most of his undertakings, was impressed that he did not interfere in Greece in December 1944. 'I believe', he observed to Eden, 'that we shall gain influence with him and strengthen a moderate policy for the Soviets by showing them how our mind works.' And it was in this spirit that Churchill went to Yalta. Only after the promises of Yalta failed to be realized did the Prime Minister change his mind. This distrust was not a one-sided affair. Stalin was equally doubtful about his Western Allies. Misunderstandings aroused by the planned meeting at Berne between Allied representatives and General Wolff, Chief of the SS in Italy, to discuss an end to hostilities on the Italian front produced a violent reaction in Moscow. Stalin sent a telegram to Roosevelt which implied that the Western Powers were about to make a separate peace with Hitler and that Kesselring* had agreed to lay down his arms on the Western front and so allow Anglo-American troops to advance into Germany while the German armies continued to fight the Russians in the East. Under such conditions unanimity of strategic purpose amongst the Allies was not readily to hand. Nor was it simply a question of differences between the Russians on the one hand and the Anglo-Americans on the other. The two last named were equally at odds.

In making final arrangements to finish off the campaign Eisenhower was influenced most of all by his overriding desire to do it with minimum casualties. Convinced, and he cannot be faulted here, that there would be no surrender while Hitler remained at the head of affairs, he was persuaded by his intelligence staffs on meagre evidence that Hitler's most likely choice when he found himself at the last gasp would be to retire with a band of fanatical die-hards to the so-called National Redoubt or Alpine Fortress in the mountains near Berchtesgaden, and there, supported by secret weapons, laugh a siege to scorn. Thus, right about the fight to death, wrong about where it would be, Eisenhower took his eye off Berlin. 'Military factors,' he maintained,

*Since 10 March Commander-in-Chief, West.

'when the enemy was on the brink of final defeat, were more important in my eyes than the political considerations involved in an Allied capture of the capital ... [which] no longer represented a military objective of major importance.' Here we come face to face with definition. What is a military objective?

Sometimes it has been a mere bridge, forage that would keep an army fed, oil, a town, communications. Sometimes it has been a whole military force; sometimes a king. The death of Richard ended the battle of Bosworth. In 1945 the target of the Allied armies was no longer the armies opposed to them. There was a much smaller and simpler key to turn off hostilities and bring peace back to Europe. The key was in Berlin, in the Bunker, in the person of the Führer himself. What an ironic twist that while all the argument was going on about Berlin's military and political significance, those arguing failed to see that Berlin itself held until the very end the only thing which kept Germany at war. Once again, as at Bosworth, it was the person of a tyrant which kept that tyrant's armies in the field, and so the tyrant had to be brought down. The grand finale of the Third Reich had already been advertised. It had all been written down in *Mein Kampf,* discussed with and made known to the world by Rauschning. *Götterdämmerung* had been reiterated a thousand times. But all this notwithstanding, Eisenhower did not see it and accordingly made his plans.

They were these. Bradley, with the bulk of Allied strength concentrated under his hand, would make a huge central drive towards Leipzig-Dresden to split Germany in half and join up with the Red Army. Then the Allied armies would branch out. One group would thrust north-east to the Baltic, another south-west to seize the National Redoubt. Churchill took an immediate dislike to this plan. First, it denied the British a leading part in the final advance; second and more disturbing, it ignored what he regarded as the biggest need of all – the capture of Berlin. Berlin in Churchill's eyes was a political objective of first importance. It was one of several instances in which the Prime Minister and the Führer thought alike. Hitler recognized and shortly before his death prophesied that the future struggle for Europe would be between Soviet Russia and the United States. Churchill agreed. Moreover he foresaw that an end to German military power would completely transform the wartime light in which the Soviet Union had looked upon her Allies. Only a common enemy could unite two such irreconcilable systems. Remove that enemy and they would once more look upon each other as enemies. Therefore, argued Churchill, well before the event, since there was to be a new confrontation between two new rivals, this confrontation should start as far east in Europe as possible. For this reason, if for no other, Berlin was a 'prime and true objective of the Anglo-American armies'. Those who seek to prolong the present status quo in Europe would do well to ask themselves whether the aims of Soviet Russia in 1974 – security on their own terms – are all that different from what they were in 1945 and might reflect too that whereas Stalin held back from time to time 'because we have no navy', that particular deficiency in the Soviet Armoury has been filled to overflowing. Churchill told the British Chiefs of Staff just what his concern was:

> It seems to me that the chief criticism of the new Eisenhower plan is that it shifts the axis of the main advance upon Berlin to the direction through Leipzig to Dresden, and thus raises the question of whether the Twenty-first Army Group will not be so stretched as to lose its offensive power, especially after it has been deprived of the Ninth United States Army. Thus we might be condemned to an almost static role in the north and virtually prevented from crossing the Elbe until an altogether later stage in the operations has been reached. All prospect of the British entering Berlin with the Americans is ruled out ... it also seems that General Eisenhower may be wrong in supposing Berlin to be largely devoid of military and political importance. Even though German Government departments have to a great extent moved to the south, the dominating fact on German minds of the fall of Berlin should not be overlooked. The idea of neglecting Berlin and leaving it to the Russians to take at a later stage does not appear to me correct. As long as Berlin holds out and withstands a siege in the ruins, as it may easily do, German resistance will be stimulated. The fall of Berlin might cause nearly all Germans to despair ...

Frederick the Great had not, of course, despaired even at the fall of Berlin. The last of Germany's War Lords did not allow Berlin's fall to precede his own, but had he been elsewhere at the time of his capital's capture it may be doubted whether he would have allowed it to bring him to despair. For despair was not in Hitler's make up.

Stalin's reaction to Eisenhower's plan, so different from Churchill's, simply redoubled the Prime Minister's instinctive disinclination to allow Berlin to fall into the hands of the Red Army. Stalin positively embraced the new plan since it 'entirely coincides with the plan of the Soviet High Command'. Berlin, declared Stalin, had lost its former strategic importance and therefore only secondary Soviet forces would

be directed against it – a statement which prompted Churchill to write
that events hardly provided corroboration. In any case it was not as if
Churchill was trying to effect fundamental changes in what Eisenhower proposed to do. He was merely saying that the course of action
already agreed upon should be stuck to. 'I should greatly prefer', his
message of 31 March to the Supreme Commander read,

> persistence in the plan on which we crossed the Rhine, namely, that
> the Ninth US Army should march with the Twenty-first Army
> Group to the Elbe and beyond Berlin. This would not be in any way
> inconsistent with the great central thrust which you are now so
> rightly developing as the result of the brilliant operations of your
> armies south of the Ruhr. It only shifts the weight of one army to the
> northern flank.

But Eisenhower had his way. He too argued that he was doing no more
than reverting to his original idea – to make one great thrust to the
East after the Ruhr had been taken in order to capture both the bulk of
what was left of the enemy's industrial capacity and the area to which
the German administrative machinery was moving. The fault in Eisenhower's reasoning was the oldest of military faults. He was pursuing the
wrong objective. He was still thinking of how to remove from Germany
the ultimate means to wage war. His mind was still on the defeat of the
Wehrmacht. It was not this defeat that Churchill was concerned with.
To his way of thinking this had already been accomplished even
though the final act of surrender was still to come. It was the link-up
with Russia *after* the war which worried Churchill. What he wanted to
know was who would get to the Baltic first, who would control the
Atlantic ports. As we have seen the pity of it was that a single objective,
Berlin, held the key both to the final demise of the Führer and thus the
war's end *and* a strong bargaining position for future dealings with
Russia.

So it might be argued that at the very end when Eisenhower at last
went for a single powerful thrust, he did so with the wrong target. At
long last he had got the tactics right, but not the strategy. He was not
alone in thinking his choice of objective was the right one. Bradley, an
excellent tactician but no strategist, spoke contemptuously of the British
desire to 'complicate the war with political foresight and non-military
objectives'. Yet as late as the first week of April Eisenhower was still
toying with the idea of changing his mind and in a signal to Marshall
admitting that the purpose of the war was to realize political aims,
offered to alter his plans and take Berlin if the Combined Chiefs of

Staff thought it proper. Whether he could have done so is another thing. But on 11 April the armoured spearheads of 9th US Army were over the Elbe near Magdeburg, a mere 50 miles from Berlin, at a time when Zhukov's forces had not even resumed the offensive and would not do so for a further five days.

At almost the twelfth hour Churchill still urged his view that the German capital was unique in its importance. He even appealed to the dying Roosevelt. But Marshall and his military men were as before obsessed with the mythical Redoubt and turned their faces aside from political realities. Eisenhower's final orders required Allied forces to halt on the general line of the Elbe and Mulde except for Montgomery's group of armies which pressed on to the Baltic. With this single last exception the orders could not have better suited the Red Army. The glittering prize, however tarnished it might be by bombing and artillery, the great political plum of Berlin was not for the plucking by Eisenhower or Montgomery. It was into Zhukov's hand that it would fall.

Here then is the business of our two hours' traffic on the battlefield and at the conference table. Decisions made at one would determine and themselves be determined by decisions made at the other.

2

THE THIRD REICH
AT BAY

*As long as there was a man left in Prussia, that man might
carry a musket; as long as there was a horse left, that horse
might draw artillery ... while the means of sustaining and
destroying life remained, Frederic was determined to fight it
out to the very last.*

MACAULAY

At the beginning of 1945 the strategic situation of the Third Reich was
without hope. The initiative which Hitler had enjoyed for so long with
such cruel consequences had gone for ever, and Germany's enemies by
land, sea and air were closing in for the kill. But the leader of Germany
had never learned to know the word 'capitulation', and so the struggle
for Europe went on. Plans for resolving this struggle made by both sets
of contestants were – like so many grand strategic designs of past and
present – more to be compared with the baseless fabric of Prospero's
vision, more the stuff as dreams are made on, than the *quod erat
demonstrandum* arrived at by calculated consideration of military
facts. Yet these facts delivered a plain message.

No message was spelled out more clearly than that concerning the
total incapacity of Germany to meet on anything like tolerable terms
the threat she faced from Allied air forces, particularly in the West.
This point is perhaps most strikingly illustrated when we consider that
a great concentration of German air strength there did not alter her
condition of helplessness. On the last day of 1944 the Luftwaffe had
deployed the great bulk of its fighters in the West either in direct
support of the armies or for air defence. More than three-quarters of
the total number of its day fighters – some 2,300 – and all but a few of
its 1,300 night fighters were there. In addition to this, nearly a
million of the Wehrmacht's men were eaten up by anti-aircraft

defences. Yet on that same day, 31 December 1944 – and needless to say starting many hours before dawn in the protective darkness – Albert Speer, Minister of Armament and War Production, drove from the headquarters of General Sepp Dietrich at Houffalize in the Ardennes to Führer HQ at Bad Nauheim – a distance of 200 miles. The journey took him twenty two hours. Why was he required to proceed at less than 10 miles an hour? Because again and again he was obliged to stop and scurry for cover from fighter planes – this with most of the Luftwaffe positioned in that very sector. Before setting off from Headquarters 6 Panzer Army Speer's talk with Dietrich had constantly been interrupted by low level bombing attacks from massed United States Air Force formations – which together with stubborn American defence and Eisenhower's call on substantial reserves had spelled ruin to the Ardennes counter offensive. 'Howling and exploding bombs, clouds illuminated in red and yellow hues, droning motors, and no defence anywhere – I was stunned', writes Speer, 'by this scene of military impotence which Hitler's miscalculations had given such a grotesque setting.'

So total a relinquishment of control of the air did not mean simply that the German troops and vehicles, supply dumps and communications were hammered from the air. It meant too that these same troops and vehicles could not *move* – at least not in the tactical sense, not in such a way that the traditional advantage of interior lines of communication, Germany's central strategic position, could be enjoyed and exploited. Mobility – which together with fire power is the foundation of all success in war – was gone and with it all capacity for any military action other than reaction to Allied initiatives. There was no question any more of switching reserves rapidly from one front to another, of cutting down first an enemy in the East, then turning back to do the same in the West. This loss of adaptability imposed by Allied air power plus Hitler's own rejection of what adaptability was still open to him, that is to say his insistence on holding on to what could not be held on to and thus dispersing his not inconsiderable military strength, guaranteed the impotence which Speer had referred to.

Reluctance to face the truth which the various conquerors of Europe have always shown when the moment came for drawing in their horns never ceases to astonish, not only in its repetition, but in its utter incompatibility with those very principles whose application made possible their conquests in the first place. Yet explanation for this stubborn insistence on failure, however unsatisfactory, is not hard to find. Apart from the political consequences inherent in withdrawal, it often springs from a constitutional dislike of playing the waiting game. Wellington had always maintained of Napoleon that he lacked the patience for defensive operations. And toward the end when in March 1814 the Emperor was vainly trying to resist the combined advances of the Prussians under Blücher and the Austrians under Schwarzenberg, when he had need of every soldier, gun and horse he could lay his hands on, he left 70,000 veterans to guard the Rhine fortresses. Not only was he trying 'to retain the unretainable', but even their retention could have had no effect on the progress of the war, which by that time was moving to the heart of his Empire – Paris. What Napoleon had done on the small scale, Hitler did on the grand, and in a similar vein, a similar refusal to acknowledge facts and be patient, Hitler would fly into a temper every time one of his generals discussed the operational need for this or that. He would always equate the word 'operational' with withdrawal. By refusing to have any truck with operational needs, he refused also to allow for any alternative except withdrawal. While reiterating to the point of tedium that history was not going to be repeated, that there would never be any surrender, that he would fight until five minutes past twelve and so on, while insisting on every effort being made to ensure the successful defence of the Reich, he insisted as well on taking those steps which were best designed to weaken his defences, speed the hands round the clock and make inevitable the very surrender which was not to be contemplated.

All this contradictory claptrap was contained in the lecture Hitler gave to his generals on 28 December 1944 on the eve of his offensive in Alsace. During this conference – if conference is the right word for what on the one hand was largely a monologue painting a picture of a fictional world, making both a statement of intentions and an exhortation to still greater effort, and what on the other hand was a response whose outward loyalty concealed despair and disillusion – Hitler in one more colossal fabrication of untruths deceived himself on two counts, first as to the local situation on the Western front, second in referring more generally to the future conduct of the war. On the first count the Ardennes offensive had transformed the situation (as indeed it had – but not in the way Hitler meant), a tremendous easing had taken place, the Allies were off balance, had eaten up all their reserves, abandoned all their offensive plans, and all that was needed now was simply to knock away half the enemy's Western front merely by annihilating the American divisions one by one. There was a good deal more trash of this sort, and the Führer reserved his greatest flights of self-deception not for what had happened, but for his generalizations about what was still to come.

Once this elimination of the Americans had taken place, Hitler claimed that a further 45 German divisions would be ready and in the long run the enemy would never be able to resist these extra forces. Where these 45 divisions were to come from was not made known, yet the absurdity of the whole strategic situation was that Hitler could have put his hands on more than 45 divisions if he had chosen to cut his losses, forget about irrelevant sideshows and concentrate his forces on the one thing that really mattered – the defence of Germany. In his own words to the generals at the same conference on 28 December he put his finger on the key point of his strategic dilemma : 'we should not forget that even today we are defending an area . . . which is essentially larger than Germany has ever been, and that there is at our disposal an armed force which even today is unquestionably the most powerful on earth.' It was precisely this – the size of the area being defended – which made even the most powerful armed force on earth (a claim itself insupportable if we think of no more than the Red Army plus Anglo/American air and naval forces) inadequate. At this time Hitler had 260 divisions in the field. Their distribution reflected Hitler's claim about the area to be defended and at the same time illustrated how strategically frail and vulnerable Germany's whole position was. In the West were 76 divisions, in Italy 24, 10 were in Yugoslavia, 17 in Scandinavia. In the East were 133 divisions – but of these only 75 were in the vital area of East Prussia and Poland – the remainder were dispersed in guarding strategic trifles. Some 30 divisions were cut off in Courland and Memel; a similar number were struggling to check the Russian advance in Hungary. If we now consider for one moment the strength which could be mustered against this German deployment we can at once detect its fatal flaw. Eisenhower's groups of armies numbered some 78 divisions (that is a similar number to that opposing him) while on the Eastern front in Poland alone, according to Stalin, the Russians had about 180.

If instead of a policy of hanging on everywhere, Hitler had concentrated on essentials, we might imagine a deployment which guarded against its greatest and most immediate dangers, that is one to keep the Western Allies at arms length on the Rhine and the Apennines, concentrate every available division against the Red Army *and* maintain a substantial reserve, a deployment which disposed the 260 divisions with say 100 on the Western front and in Italy, and all the rest – for stemming the Red Army. If this had been done, Guderian when discussing the situation with Hitler on 9 January 1945 would have had no need to describe the Eastern front as a house of cards. Why was it then that Hitler had rejected a deployment most likely to wrest advantage from the military probabilities? The answer lay in his last-minute hopes – not of staving off defeat – but of snatching victory at the twelfth hour, snatching it by means of new air and sea weapons.

It must always remain a disagreeable reflection that had Hitler given the right people the right instructions at the right time, he might have been in possession of nuclear weapons – deliverable either by jet aircraft or submarine rockets – well before the Western Allies. That he would not have hesitated to use them goes without saying. Fortunately like all dilettantes in the art and science of war he was unable to concentrate on one thing at a time or to see that for the first time in the history of the world a single weapon could be more powerful and more decisive than all the soldierly virtues of the Master Race. Speer has recorded how his master's imagination would flit from scheme to scheme and never settle on one.

In September 1943 while Speer was at Rechlin, the Luftwaffe test site, for an armaments congress, he was shown a telegram by Field Marshal Milch, armaments chief of the Luftwaffe. It was an order from Hitler to put a stop to the arrangements for producing on a large scale the Me-262, Germany's most up to date fighter which had two jet engines, a speed of more than 500 mph and thus a great combat superiority over any other fighter possessed by either side. Yet within a few months and because he had heard that British experiments with jet aircraft were meeting with some success, Hitler reversed his decision. It should perhaps be added here that as early as 1941 Professor Heinkel was testing his first jet engines. Having reversed his earlier decision – a step at least in the right direction – Hitler completely spoiled it by laying down that the Me-262 would be used – not as a fighter, but as a fast bomber. The absurdity of this decision, that is to say giving up the potential not merely of being able to take on the Allied bomber forces with every advantage of speed and manoeuvrability, but also able to outfly the Allied fighters, is only explained when we remember that defensive measures and the patient waiting game had no appeal for Hitler. It was attack and the offensive which fascinated him. It was this same obsession with taking the initiative which influenced him in altering the course of Germany's rocket missile policy. The ground-to-air missiles might have had a major effect on stopping the terrible blows aimed at German industry and thus the Wehrmacht's offensive capability by the Allied air forces. But this too was a defensive measure and therefore to be jettisoned. Instead the V2 missile was to hit directly at England. 'The whole notion was absurd', wrote Speer. 'Fleets of enemy bombers in 1944 were dropping an average of 3,000 tons of bombs a day over a span of several months. And Hitler wanted to retaliate with 30 rockets which would have carried 24 tons of explosives to England daily.' Yet this was typical of Hitler. He would rather accept 3,000 tons a day on Germany and console himself that he was hitting back than try to do away with the need to accept bombs falling on his own country. Thus his lust for destruction, even nihilistic self-destruction, found expression. It is more easy to understand when we consider the new U-boat, for here was a weapon which might have enabled Hitler to regain and keep the initiative in at least one element.

Admiral Dönitz, when early in 1943 he succeeded Raeder as Commander-in-Chief of the German Navy (and who was even to succeed Hitler as Führer for a week), had insisted that only the new type of U-boat would be any good for continuing to wage submarine warfare, that is the genuine U-boat which remained submerged and had a speed of 15 knots – greater than that of most targets, the Allied merchantmen, and even some of their hunters, the escorts. In July 1943 Otto Nerker, whom Speer chose to run the project, had worked out a production system. It was the prefabrication method. The boats would be built inland, moved by their various parts to the shipyards and then assembled there. In December 1943 Speer and Dönitz inspected the first wooden mock-up of the new U-boat, and asked themselves why they had not begun building them earlier. 'No technical innovations were employed,' Speer observes, 'the engineering principles had been known for years, and the new boats would have revolutionized submarine warfare.' As it was the first boats were not delivered until 1944, and as Speer also noted had it not been for Allied aircraft destroying a third of the submarines built when they were at the dockyards, 40 a month would have been produced by the beginning of 1945. It was just as well they were not for anything that combined the technologically revolutionary with the violently aggressive fitted exactly with Hitler's ideas of waging political or military warfare. Yet it was this desire for such weapons that obliged Hitler to hang on to the other more strategically irrelevant areas – for example North Sea and Baltic naval bases for the U-boats, and the V2 launching areas in Holland. At a naval conference on 3 January 1945 Dönitz made matters worse by insisting on the need to hang on to Courland, Memel and the Gulf of Danzig – Guderian had already tried to persuade Hitler to withdraw from there and was to go on doing so until it was too late – in order to have U-boat bases and work-up areas out of range of Allied aircraft. So for the sake of a delusion, the notion that the new U-boat would actually change the course of the war, an infinitely precious number of divisions was chucked away and unable to contribute anything to the one real and critical strategic requirement – defence of the Reich itself.

It is strange that Hitler showed so little interest in the possibility of an atomic bomb. If ever there was a weapon which epitomized the revolutionary and the violent, here it was. But, says Speer, 'the idea quite obviously strained his intellectual capacity; he was unable to grasp the revolutionary nature of nuclear physics'. Only once in all the conferences which Speer had with Hitler was nuclear fission mentioned and then only briefly. Speer adds however that he was sure that Hitler would not have hesitated for a moment to employ atom bombs against England. We may be grateful for incalculably large mercies.

Meanwhile as the last year of the war began, the Allies were showing no mercy towards the Third Reich. And the truth was that for Hitler the war at sea was lost, the war in the air was lost and the war on land was about to be lost. That all three wars were closely interrelated – were indeed one war – goes without saying. In drawing attention to this point and to the grotesque measures to which Hitler was forced to resort by virtue of having to fight on two fronts, Chester Wilmot had this to add : 'Because the German Air Force was unable to protect the U-boat bases and training waters in the Western Baltic, the German Army was obliged to hold the Eastern Baltic against the Russians so that the German Navy might build up a new U-boat fleet capable of inflicting a severe defeat on the Western Allies, and especially on the hated British whose refusal to capitulate in 1940 had made inevitable the war on two fronts which had already destroyed most of Hitler's empire and was in the process of destroying the Third Reich.' It would be hard to substitute a more succinct analysis of the strategic pickle which Hitler's policies had brought about.

The German Air Force's impotence was not confined to the Western Baltic. As we have seen from Speer's recollections during the latter stages of the Ardennes offensive, it was impotent in two other aspects – in the direct support of the German armies either in respect of aiming blows at Allied ground forces or warding off blows aimed at them by Allied air forces, and in the defence of Germany itself. Quite clearly the closer the Allied Armies got to Germany, the closer too were drawn together tactical air operations in direct support of those armies and the more remote strategic air offensive aimed at the enemy sinews

Winter warfare on the Eastern Front

Winter warfare on the Western Front

of war. In December 1944, for example, of the nearly 85,000 tons of bombs dropped on to enemy targets by the United States Air Force and the RAF, little short of one half were delivered in support of the Ardennes battles.

Controversy as to the most profitable use of air power persisted until and beyond the end of the war in Europe. By the end of 1944 the effect of Allied air superiority had made itself felt in a number of ways. It may be doubted whether Operation *Overlord* could have been mounted at all without it; the decisive Allied victory in Normandy was due in large measure to air power; Hitler's Ardennes offensive received its death blow from the air; German industry, supplies of new material and communications had all suffered crippling blows. Yet those who had maintained that strategic air power alone could weaken the German nation to the point where armed resistance would no longer be possible had not enjoyed the satisfaction of seeing this argument borne out by events. The general purpose of the Allied strategic air offensive was threefold – progressively to destroy and disrupt the whole German war making machine with its military, industrial and economic components; to dislocate communications to the point where their state would significantly complement the first objective; and, of course, to render the Luftwaffe incapable of interfering with their programme. From time to time more particular objectives had to take priority over this general purpose – for example the need to ensure that *Overlord* – in so far as getting a firm foothold in Normandy was concerned – succeeded. As we know, it did, and the two sorts of objective, general and particular, were inter-dependent. While the general aim of subduing the German air force to the point where it could no longer offer resistance had not been achieved by long range bomber forces alone, other influences were at work. *Overlord* with its actual capture of territory and consequent overrunning of German airfields and early warning systems, together with the ability to deploy a greater bulk of Allied bombers on advanced airfields plus better methods of attack – all these things contributed to the achievement of the general aim.

Talk of bringing Germany to her knees by lack of oil alone was, of course, so much trash – yet the results achieved by strategic bombing were remarkable, and had they been maintained, could even have been conclusive. For example between April and September 1944 Germany's total production of aviation fuel fell from 175,000 tons to the tiny figure of 9,400. Yet by November it was back at 41,000. And although great reductions in other sorts of fuel and armaments production had also been achieved, German production of guns and ammunition between the summer and winter of 1944 remained extraordinarily steady – this in spite of the fact that with the Normandy victory complete, the bulk of strategic air forces returned to their traditional, that is their general, targets. Bad weather alone could not explain this failure to deal a decisive blow. Bad planning was to blame as well.

The essence of a good military plan is that you should choose the right objective and then allot the necessary resources for its achievement. In both requirements, to start with at least, the Allies were not quite up to the job. Disagreement as to objectives centred round the respective virtues of oil targets, German morale and support of land forces. In an attempt to compromise with a single type of target which would encompass all needs, General Arnold, commanding us Army Air Forces, recommended that efforts should be concentrated on the German transport system. Air Chief Marshal Harris, commanding Bomber Command, disagreed and insisted that area bombing was of all methods the most deadly. Equally controversial was the question of command – should it be invested in the Combined Chiefs of Staff, which with delegation to the British Chief of Air Staff and the Commander us Air Forces would mean a divided command. Nonetheless this was what was done, with a broad directive that both the German military, industrial and economic systems *and* direct support of land operations should represent the mission of the combined air forces.

Failure to concentrate on a single objective led to indecisive results. Oil targets, marshalling yards, area bombing, support of land operations – all received attention. But after the establishment of a Combined Strategic Targets Committee and further discussion as to the respective merits of the various targets, it was decided in the autumn of 1944 to concentrate in the main part on two – oil and transport, transport being in this sense another name for communications. In November 1944 the former received 30,000 tons, the latter 20,000 tons. Steadily these two received more and more of the total weight. As Speer contemplated the Allied programme, he predicted 'complete disaster and general catastrophe'. At last the Allies had hit on a formula which would ensure that Hitler's war machine could not go on functioning much longer.

That communications and transport were indeed absolutely key factors in the determination of conflict on a world scale was borne out by the fact that there had never been a time when Allied communications and transport had not been their Achilles heel. Unlike the Germans' these communications and transports were at sea. As early as the spring of 1940 General Wavell had set down in a general estimate of the strategic situation that oil, shipping, air and sea power were indispensable to victory, and that since the British had a lot of shipping, naval power, potentially great air power and thus access to nearly all the world's oil, the Allies were bound to win. Yet in the battle of the Atlantic they came perilously close to losing, and even though by 1943, the battle of the Atlantic had been won, it was, unlike some battles on land, a battle which could never be won finally, until all German naval power was in Allied hands. This meant that the Allies, by not capturing all German naval bases in 1944, had still to face a threat at sea in 1945. In December 1944 the U-boat fleet was thought to number almost 200 operational boats with a further 128 in training. What was not known was how many of the new fast under-water boats would make their appearance. In the event none did, but the last of Dönitz's U-boat offensives, although it could not change the course of the war, inflicted grave losses on Allied shipping – over a quarter of a million tons with about half as much again accounted for by other means – surface vessels (notably the E boats) mines and aircraft. Command of the sea, although largely enjoyed by the Allies, was thus not absolute even near the end.

Still less absolute was their domination of the land battle. On New Year's Day 1945, a day traditionally of good omen in German military history, Hitler launched yet one more offensive in the West – this time in Alsace, when eight divisions attacked from the Saar, west and east of the Vosges, against Devers' 6th Army Group. Further north Bradley's and Montgomery's Army Groups were still struggling in appalling weather to push back the Ardennes bulge. There was as yet no walk-over in the West. In the south the 5th US and 8th British Armies under Alexander's overall command were still stuck on the winter line south of Bologna and would not make a move for months to come. In the East the battle line passed through Yugoslavia south of Sarajevo, Czechoslovakia, in Hungary west of Budapest, the line of the Oder and eastwards through East Prussia. In the East too there was a lull, but it was about to become an avalanche. While Hitler was seeking by all and every means to stave off defeat, his head whirling with fantastic ideas about how the new weapons would come to his rescue, about how to inflict a defeat on the Western Allies and come to terms with them, above all how so to arrange things that the honour of the nation would not be besmirched, an honourable peace secured that would last 50 or 100 years, while his will was insisting before all else that he would never give in, the allies were sticking to their formula of 'Unconditional Surrender' and making their plans to bring it about.

Eisenhower's plan, sent to Montgomery on 31 December 1944, was broadly to destroy all enemy forces to the west of the Rhine (north of the Moselle) and to prepare to cross the Rhine in strength with the main thrust north of the Ruhr. There were to be several phases. The first job was to remove the Ardennes salient which had been made by Model's group of three German armies including two Panzer Armies 5th and 6th, and this was to be done by converging attacks from north and south. The seriousness with which the Supreme Allied Commander still regarded the Ardennes situation was made clear by his references to the determined efforts still being made by the enemy with his mobile forces. 'Therefore,' wrote Eisenhower, 'we must be prepared to use everything consistent with minimum security requirements to accomplish their destruction.' That he regarded the Ardennes as the danger spot was further emphasized by his noting that what must be prevented above all was the enemy's attempting to stabilize the Ardennes bulge with infantry, thus freeing the Panzer divisions for use anywhere else that they might choose. 'We must regain the initiative,' he urged, 'speed and energy are essential.' That it should have been necessary to write such things is the best possible evidence that, in the West at least all was not over bar the shouting and that some of the things which Hitler had claimed for his offensive were all too accurate.

Once the Ardennes salient had been eliminated, however, and the initiative properly back in Allied hands, plans for the resumption of what had always been Eisenhower's strategy, that is to advance on a broad front, were concerned with the first part of his general directive – to close up to the Rhine. The US 1st Army – under Montgomery's command for the Ardennes battle – would revert to Bradley whose 12th Army Group would then drive north-east on the line Prüm-Bonn. Montgomery's 21st Army Group with 9th US Army still under command would clear the area from the Maas and Roer to the Rhine roughly between Düsseldorf and Emmerich. Priority for US reinforcements would go to Bradley, but additionally it was Eisenhower's intention once more to build up his reserves – frittered away in containing the Ardennes offensive – in order to exploit what success he had. Nonetheless, so concerned still were some Allied leaders about German pressure in the West and indeed about the whole question of whether Eisenhower's strategy would succeed, that Churchill sent a telegram to Stalin on 6 January 1945, to find out whether Russian plans were likely to include an offensive on the Eastern front to facilitate attack by Montgomery's and Bradley's Army Groups. In his telegram Churchill pointed out how heavy the battle in the West was and that it was a time for grave decision. Referring to the difficulties of recapturing the initiative when conducting defensive operations on a very wide front, he stressed the need for Eisenhower to have some notion of Russian plans which would be likely to have major effects on his own. Therefore, Churchill wanted to know 'whether we can count on a major Russian offensive on the Vistula front or elsewhere during January'.

Stalin's reply was immediate and encouraging. Stressing the need to take full advantage of the Red Army's superiority in artillery and their overall armament advantage in the air, he was specific about the Soviet intention to mount a major attack as soon as possible. Despite the need for clear weather, despite the fact that the weather was at that time (7 January) bad, and 'taking into account the position of our Allies on the Western Front, GHQ of the Supreme Command has decided to accelerate the completion of our preparations, and, regardless of the weather, to commence large-scale offensive operations against the Germans along the whole Central Front not later than the second half of January'. Thus was Eisenhower reassured.

Never was the impossibility of fighting a successful war on two fronts with inadequate resources better illustrated than by the dramatic sweep of events between January and April 1945. Very broadly while the Western armies closed up to the Rhine slowly and laboriously during January and February and the Russians swept across the frozen plains of Poland gaining hundreds of miles, after that time, roles were reversed and in March and April the Red Army was stuck on the Oder-Neisse line, while Eisenhower's troops advanced headlong into Germany. The Russians themselves, however, had foreseen no such setback.

As early as November 1944 plans had been made to take the Red Army from the Vistula to the Oder and on to Berlin itself. There had even been a series of war games to prepare for the actual operation and Lieutenant-General Antipenko, who was Zhukov's chief of rear services or logistics, has described how Zhukov conducted it. Zhukov himself was by this time in command of the 1st Belorussian *front*, this being the group of armies which was to be directed towards Berlin. Between 8 and 10 December Zhukov held his war game in which all army commanders and heads of services participated. The actual operational plans were played during the game, so that all problems of tactics, movement, artillery, air support, bridges, mine clearance, road building, hospitals, supplies, logistics and so on could be studied in time to find sensible solutions for them. To give an idea of the scale of the planned offensive, we should bear in mind that of the seven Soviet *fronts* positioned facing the German forces no fewer than four were involved – Zhukov's 1st Belorussian, Konev's 1st Ukrainian, Rokossovsky's 2nd Belorussian and Petrov's 4th Ukrainian. Of these the spearheads were to be Zhukov's and Konev's *fronts*, and these alone contained the staggering total of two and a quarter million men, nearly 5,000 aircraft, 32,000 guns and mortars, 6,500 tanks – a total of more than 160 divisions.

The broad objective of this so-called *Vistula-Oder* Operation was to liberate Poland, destroy the Wehrmacht's Army Group A, reach the Oder and prepare to take Berlin. It was also – and here we find Stalin's promise reflected – 'to divert enemy forces from the West European front and to ease the situation for the American and British armies which had developed in connection with the offensive by the German fascist troops in the Ardennes and the Vosges.' In general outline there would be two great *Schwerpunkte*, one aimed at Poznan, one at Breslau, and between them the defending German troops would be isolated and crushed in detail. Would Army Group A be in a position to avoid this bleak prospect?

What was the German position on the Eastern front? Guderian, as Chief of the General Staff, at a time when Hitler was still directing the Ardennes and Alsace battles from his Ziegenberg *Eagle's Nest*, was responsible for day-to-day operations in the East and as he has recorded, he was far from sanguine. On 25 December 1944 Guderian received at Zossen, HQ OKH, an unwelcome Christmas greeting, to the effect that Hitler had decided to move General Gille's SS Panzer Corps from General Reinhardt's Army Group Centre, that is from the area north of Warsaw, to Budapest – in other words away from the area where the colossal Russian blow was about to be delivered. This reduced the reserves to a dangerously low level, only $12\frac{1}{2}$ mobile divisions for a front of 750 miles. So disturbed was he that, after conferring with Gehlen* (about whom a good many books have recently been published, including his own *Der Dienst*), Guderian was convinced that only a transfer of main defensive strength to the East would have a chance of holding the Russians. He set off on New Year's Eve to see

---

*It is revealing to note that Gehlen considers Hitler's decision to invade the Soviet Union not merely correct but inevitable. It was with Hitler's method of conducting the campaign that Gehlen found fault, not the idea of the campaign itself.

Hitler once more, and having discussed matters with Commander-in-Chief West, von Rundstedt, and his Chief of Staff, Westphal, managed to discover that some four divisions could in their view be made available. Thus armed, he confronted Jodl and succeeded in getting their transfer agreed – but only to have them re-transferred on Hitler's orders to Hungary, where the German counter-attack to relieve Budapest with these additional forces failed. Then from 5–8 January Guderian either visited or telephoned his Army Group Commanders, Harpe, Army Group A, Reinhardt, Army Group Centre, Wöhler, Army Group South. As a result Guderian concluded that two things were necessary – minor tactical withdrawals by Reinhardt and Harpe in order to shorten their lines and reconstitute a reserve and a further transfer of forces from the Western front. He therefore returned to *Eagle's Nest* on 9 January. When Hitler saw Gehlen's appreciation of enemy strength and intentions, he pronounced them to be completely idiotic and ordered that Gehlen himself be shut up in a lunatic asylum. Guderian managed to evade this instruction, but even so, he got neither permission to withdraw nor any reinforcements. 'The Eastern front must help itself and make do with what it's got.' No wonder Guderian described this front as a house of cards which with so few reserves would collapse everywhere if penetrated anywhere. Reinhardt made a similar comment after hearing what sort of strength the Russians were likely to have available for their attack so that the blows they would deliver would not merely be heavy, but would succeed each other almost endlessly. 'By the time the last one comes,' he observed, '. . . we shall be debris.'

There were sound reasons for thinking so. The superiority of men and machines which the Russians enjoyed was overwhelming, far more than the traditional three to one always regarded as the minimum required for successful attack. In the critical central area the Russians had more than five times as many soldiers, eight times as many guns and mortars, six times as many tanks and nearly eighteen times as many aircraft as the Germans. The Russian official account, *History of the Great Patriotic War of the Soviet Union*,* contains a restrained comment on how auspicious the strategic situation was for the Russians in the Central section of the front before the battle began :

Having a great advantage over the enemy troops and occupying favourable positions for the offensive, the Soviet armed forces firmly held the initiative in their hands. The enemy, though he also had

Istoriya Velikoy Otechestvennoy Voiny Sovetskogo Soyuza, 1941–45.

strong forces, was nevertheless unable to establish a sufficient density in artillery and tanks in the directions of the main strikes by Soviet troops.

If then the liberation of Poland and the arrival of the Red Army on the banks of the Oder was so confidently predicted, it was by no means unreal for the Russians to be talking already of the final drive on Berlin. As far back as September Eisenhower had been doing the same thing though with far less reason. In a letter to his Army Group Commanders written in the middle of that month, he had predicted that the Allies would soon be in possession of the Ruhr, the Saar and Frankfurt, and he pronounced Berlin to be the main prize. 'There is no doubt whatsoever, in my mind, that we should concentrate all our energies and resources on a rapid thrust to Berlin.' For those of us now contemplating the tragedy of the Second World War from the comfortable positions of armchairs, the next sentence of his letter contains a wealth of dramatic irony : 'Our strategy, however, will have to be coordinated with that of the Russians'. Stalemate in the autumn, the winter shock of the Ardennes, the bitter fighting to repel the German advance meant that the word Berlin did not seriously appear again in Eisenhower's planning until 20 January 1945, and this we must examine later. Before we do there are the January battles themselves to consider.

As the last year of the war began, therefore, the broad strategic situation of Germany was, as we have seen, unenviable. 'Her armies', observes the official History, 'were hard pressed, her naval and air forces were subdued, and her economy functioned with increasing strain on the basis of perpetual emergency.' Yet she did not collapse. There were many reasons for this. First and foremost was the will power of a Führer who refused, like Queen Victoria, to admit that the possibility of defeat existed, and who in any event was prepared to fight until five past twelve, to clutch at any straw, to allow the nation to be destroyed rather than surrender, and ignoring tomorrow altogether risk everything today on one turn of pitch-and-toss. As the machine, military and industrial, which sustained the continued fighting had neither exhausted all its material resources nor had run out of territorial space in which to manipulate them, organized effort was still possible. Capacity and resolution combined could still do much. But capacity was running out, and resolution by itself only served still further to squander capacity. The floodgates might be creaking; they had not yet cracked. Hitler had once said of the Soviet Union that you had only to kick in the door and the whole rotten structure would come crashing

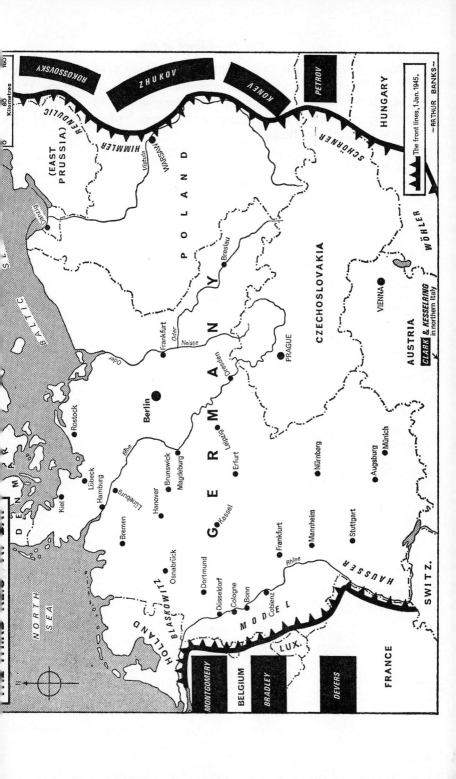

The front lines, 1 Jan. 1945.

~ARTHUR BANKS~

down. Now the Allies, West and East, were about to kick in Germany's door. The question was not whether the whole structure of the Third Reich would or would not come crashing down. The question was simply when and where. On this would depend who fought and who won the battle for Berlin.

3

JANUARY BATTLES

In the hope of gaining victory on the Meuse and recovery on the Danube, Hitler courted defeat on the Vistula.

CHESTER WILMOT

If, like Stendhal, you are determined to have a taste of war, avoid the inclement months, unless the conditions are so bad that there is no question of doing any fighting at all, but, like our far more sensible forbears of the eighteenth and seventeenth centuries, you simply occupy winter quarters. The discomfort and unpleasantness of fighting in the winter during the Second World War were compounded by the fact that battles tended to last such a tediously long time. Some forty years ago Wavell made a point to Liddell-Hart that had he had but world enough and time, he would have concentrated in his study of war on what he called actualities – 'the effects of tiredness, hunger, fear, lack of sleep, weather, inaccurate information, the time factor and so forth'. It was these things, he maintained, which made battles diffi- cult and complex, not the rules which governed strategy and tactics nor those which arranged for the sinews of war. The rules themselves were 'absurdly simple' – not so the actualities which had so profound an influence on the rules.

After three and a half years of fighting in Russia, the German Army had good reason to bear witness to the effect that cold, hunger, tired- ness and lack of sleep could have. In November and December 1941 shortly before his dismissal by Hitler, Guderian, who commanded the 2nd Panzer Army, is eloquent in his letters about the miseries of the Russian campaign. These letters abound with the actualities of war. On one occasion he refers to the bitter cold, the improbability of finding any shelter, the lack of proper clothing, the shortage of fuel, and concludes that such things made his duties a burden which almost crushed him. And then there was another actuality : command – how the armies were handled. However simple the rules might be, they could just as simply be ignored, at least by a man like Hitler. So Guderian bewails the refusal of the Supreme Command to believe these actualities and their insistence on continuing to make demands out of all proportion to the realities. They, the Supreme Command, had made no preparation for a severe winter and were actually surprised when the cold reached minus 30 degrees – a temperature in which, as Halder later observed, troops are disinclined to hold ground. The frost did not just kill and incapacitate the soldiers; it put the guns and tanks out of action too. 'The gods alone can tell how much longer we shall be able to use them in this cold.' The whole campaign in short had been based on one of the actualities Wavell referred to – inaccurate information. The Red Army, the sheer hugeness of the country, the awful weather, all had been misjudged. 'I would never have believed', Guderian concluded, 'that a really brilliant military position could be so buggered up in two months.' One of the few consolations that Guderian had was the endurance, courage and skill of those who did the actual fighting. 'Over and over again I am thankful that our men are such good soldiers.' But when Guderian represented his views to the Führer, the greatest strategic genius of all time, it simply led to his being relieved of his command.

Although there was nothing which could properly be compared with the Eastern front, those who fought in Italy or on the Western front had their share of miseries. In Italy particularly, snow, mud, ice and rain were the rule rather than the exception and as Field Marshal Alexander remembered at the end of the campaign there, the troops were always faced with 'one more mountain range or river to cross in the face of an enemy resistance which never seemed to weaken'. The Ardennes too turned on the sort of weather more associated with the North Pole than the heart of Western Europe. As Montgomery's January counter-attacks got under way, blizzards, biting winds, frozen ground, tracks too icy and slippery for even tracked vehicles to stay on, snow and fog so thick that British and German troops kept finding themselves mixed up together, sleep and hot food out of the question – it was no joke. 'The blizzard howled and raged,' wrote one veteran of the battle, 'with ever increasing intensity and not even the massive Christmas tree regalia which the fighting soldier dons in battle could in any way relieve the numbing effect of the Arctic wind.' Another soldier recalled that tanks were required to advance up icy trails, attempt to shoot and manoeuvre when blinded by fog, the men soaked, and no possibility of supply vehicles reaching them with their indispensable ammunition, food and petrol – so that all these things had to be man-handled up freezing, slippery slopes. After nearly a week's exposure to murderous enemy fire and viciously cold weather, short of sleep, food, warmth and everything that made a soldier's life tolerable, and having lost more than half its strength in killed and wounded, one battalion was nevertheless ready to fight on and was immovable by enemy counter-attack from the objectives it had so hardly won. We may conclude therefore that the actuality to dominate all others was and is the spirit of the soldier himself. And this spirit was inevitably fortified or eroded by the sort of leadership, the sort of command, under which he found himself. The Allied leadership on the Western front in January 1945 was uneven, capricious, discordant, characterized by the drive for national or personal glorification, and at times even contradictory. The truth was that the master rule of making war – however simple Wavell might have judged it – was neither clearly recognized nor properly weighed. What was it that the Anglo–us–French armies in the West were trying to do? This was the question.

On 6 December 1944, ten days before the Ardennes offensive further dismayed Allied counsels, Mr Churchill had telegraphed to President Roosevelt his concern that the gap between expectations and realities was too wide for comfort. He pointed out that the Allies had failed to achieve the strategic objectives they had set themselves on the Western front, that is to say they had not even reached the Rhine in the critical northern sector, still less established bridgeheads over it with a view to the supremely, overridingly important task of advancing into Germany. Churchill further complained that the Germans were standing firm in Italy and would in any case be able to extract their divisions there and in the Balkans for further and later defence of the Reich and that the mere condition of obstinate resistance on all European fronts had meant that Mountbatten in South-East Asia had not after all been reinforced in order to take Rangoon. This in turn had a grave effect on China's ability to persevere with the struggle against Japan. The only drops of comfort which the Prime Minister was able to find in all this sea of frustration was that the United States forces were making progress in the Pacific and that the Russians would be starting their winter campaign in the following month, January 1945. In summing up the situation and in scrutinizing those most telling of factors in war – probabilities – Churchill concluded that it was necessary to face:

    a. A considerable delay in reaching, still more in forcing, the Rhine on the shortest road to Berlin.

b. A marked degree of frustration in Italy.

c. The escape home of a large part of the German forces from the Balkan peninsula.

d. Frustration in Burma.

e. Elimination of China as a combatant.

Therefore he urged that the action necessary to resolve so unsatisfactory a state of affairs should be examined by the Combined Chiefs of Staff prior to his and Roosevelt's planned meeting in February. His cry for action fell not on deaf but on preoccupied ears. Roosevelt's reply was to the effect that despite delays, Allied strategy was developing broadly as planned. Having made these plans, he and Churchill, the Commanders-in-Chief so to speak, must now allow their subordinates to execute them. Winter weather added to their difficulties. Yet on the Western front, a break in the Allies favour must come, in Italy Alexander was keeping many Germans busy, so were the partisan forces in the Balkans, the Russians were doing their bit.* The Far Eastern situation was less rosy, it was true, but Japan's losses were such that they could not keep it up. All in all it would be better to wait and see.

In spite of this unenthusiastic response Churchill got his conference, with both Roosevelt and Stalin and the Combined Chiefs of Staff, but not until February 1945. Much was to occur before then. Execution of plans went on. But before these plans could begin to reflect Eisenhower's broad intentions to close up to the Rhine and cross it into Germany, the last faltering embers of Hitler's final offensive in the West had to be extinguished. There were two main fires which required attention: first what remained of the Ardennes bulge, at the turn of the year still not contemptible, and the newer but less serious German attack in Alsace. Not surprisingly the elimination of the Ardennes penetration proved more difficult and more costly than the stopping of another penetration further south. Yet the fact that Hitler insisted on having both guaranteed that neither could succeed.

There was still much hard fighting to be done by the Allies before they restored the Western front to what it had been before the Ardennes offensive. During the first week of January two major struggles were in progress: one was Patton's 3rd Army battling to the west of Bastogne in order to widen the salient he had driven through to

*The actual text of Roosevelt's telegram was 'The Russians seem to be doing their bit at the present time'. When we consider that the Red Army was preparing a crushing blow which was completely to transform the whole war against Germany, this was, to say no more, putting it mildly.

the town from the south and so bring ever increasing pressure on the southern flank of the Bulge; the other was Montgomery's drive with the US VII Corps and the British XXX Corps towards the key communications centre of Houffalize. There were many conditions favourable to the Germans. The intense cold – and no army on the Western front was better equipped and better trained for winter warfare than the Wehrmacht – multiplied the inherent advantage of the defender in such weather. For skilful use of mines, booby traps and entrenched positions concealed by the ever present snow is one thing. Advancing over icy roads and impassable boggy or mined country and so presenting yourself as a target is another. The appalling weather also robbed the attackers of their trump card – use of air power or at least of exploiting it both fully and immediately. Every inch of ground had to be fought for and sometimes re-fought for (some villages changed hands several times in as many days), as the Germans, more effective in withdrawal than perhaps any soldiers of the twentieth Century have ever been, wrested every benefit from the natural delaying strength of the Ardennes.

Yet not all this was sufficient to prevail. The combination of Allied riches in almost all the commodities which could turn the scales in war – seemingly inexhaustible reserves, concentrations of artillery, the ability to attack on a variety of axes, and to hammer the exposed flanks of the German penetration, and, of course, Allied air forces, which could not remain grounded all the time – was bound to drive back the Germans in the end. It is only necessary to recall that during a single month, mid-December 1944 to mid-January 1945, the Allies flew some 64,000 sorties and dropped more than 70,000 tons of bombs as part of the Ardennes battle, to see that if there were a single factor which contributed any more than others to the failure of Hitler's counter-offensive it was this very air power – a point strongly endorsed by von Rundstedt who maintained that Allied air activities had 'devastatingly contributed to the halting of the Ardennes offensive' since the resultant German inability to manoeuvre and supply their leading spearheads was what actually spelled defeat. If battles really are won by fire power and movement, the application of violence at a variety of different positions of the front, and you find that enemy aircraft have both prevented your moving at all – no petrol, no repair facilities, the road destroyed – and that even if you had been able to move, the guns, whose business it was to dispense violence, had no ammunition to fire, then we may see the force of von Rundstedt's argument. Yet despite all this, the Ardennes attack had fluttered the Allies, had for a time taken on the character and consequence of eagles in a dovecote. The same could hardly be said of the Alsace attack, which Hitler had maintained would knock away half the enemy's Western front and enable him with the mythical 45 divisions which by then would be ready to master fate.

The one principle of war which had been manipulated by the Germans with real skill and effect during the Ardennes battle – surprise – was wholly lacking in the Alsace affair. The possibility of such an attack had been anticipated by Eisenhower a few days after the Ardennes battle began when he had been obliged to stop Patton's own attacks in the area and had redeployed 3rd Army so that the southern flank of the Bulge could be attacked by it. General Patch's 7th Army was necessarily extended and deployed essentially for defensive operations. On 1 January the day the German attack began, 6th Army Group's front, of which 7th Army formed a part, was positioned roughly on the line Basle–Mulhouse–the Vosges–Strasbourg–Wissembourg–Bitche – 10 miles south of Saarbrücken, in other words more or less closed up to the Siegfried line, except for the Colmar pocket. The broad defensive concept originally laid down by Eisenhower was that if necessary Patch could withdraw to the line of the Vosges mountains even at the expense of giving up Strasbourg. Such a blow at France's honour was unthinkable to de Gaulle, and having failed to move Eisenhower, he appealed to Churchill and Roosevelt. Roosevelt was content to leave military decisions of this sort to the Supreme Commander. Churchill was not. His presence at the conference between de Gaulle and Eisenhower turned the scales. Eisenhower reversed his plan. Devers' 6th Army Group which maintained the Vosges as their main defensive line was to hang on to Strasbourg as long as doing so was consistent with the security of the Army Group as a whole. So it transpired.

In the event the German attack met with limited success. There were two main parts to it, one north and one south of Strasbourg. The northern attack employed some six divisions and succeeded in establishing a penetration between Bitche and Gambsheim, even crossing south of the River Moder but thereafter it was contained by the Americans. Further south the Germans attempted to expand the Colmar pocket towards Strasbourg but the French Corps with some US reinforcements did not merely hold the German attack. They set about eliminating the pocket itself. By early February they had succeeded and had closed up to the Rhine. In the north however this would take longer. Even so

(*top left*) *Model*
(*above*) *Guderian*

Von Rundstedt

German offensives in the West were a thing of the past. Hitler's belief in their recurrence was not.

We have seen that when Guderian visited Hitler at *Eagle's Nest* on 9 January, his requests to adjust the Eastern front and to reinforce it met with a dusty answer. The estimates and arguments he had put to the Führer dealt primarily with the military situation confronting Army Group A, commanded by Harpe, and Army Group Centre, commanded by Reinhardt. If we consider Guderian's presentation of what he believed to be the prospects facing Harpe, we may perhaps understand why Hitler flew off the handle and pronounced them to be 'completely idiotic'. They hardly fitted the picture which he himself had painted of the Eastern front a mere ten or so days before when while admitting to his assembled commanders in the West that Germany's forces were not unlimited and that mustering for an offensive in the West, an offensive designed to race over the Meuse, had involved grave risks elsewhere and they could not be equally strong everywhere. Nonetheless 'it has been possible on the whole to hold the Eastern front'. What Guderian had to say hardly fitted this comfortable and fictitious portrait of affairs. He reported that facing Army Group A were two Red Army *fronts*, the 1st Belorussian and 1st Ukrainian. Army Group A, with its headquarters at Krakow, was deployed on the general line of the River Vistula guarding the routes which led most directly into Germany. But already the Red Army had secured three bridgeheads over the Vistula – at Magnuszew, Pulawy and Baranow. The German estimate was that between these the two *fronts* opposite Army Group A, the Russians could call upon a total of two and a quarter million soldiers, between six and seven thousand tanks and SP guns and more than 30,000 artillery and mortar pieces. Added to this was the traditional privilege of the attacking side – ability to concentrate at the desired point of penetration, which meant, for example, that in the Magnuszew bridgehead alone Zhukov had crammed 400,000 troops, nearly 9,000 guns and mortars and some 1,700 tanks, more than the total resources at Harpe's disposal for his entire front. At the chosen *Schwerpunkte* of the three bridgeheads, the Russians were able to enjoy a general superiority of about 9 or 10 to 1 in men and weapons.

Such arithmetic did not move the Supreme Commander of the Wehrmacht. By this time Hitler was not interested in facts, at least not facts which contradicted his own special estimate of what was taking place. Guderian was one of the few who dared to tell the Führer what he believed to be the truth. But the truth was irrelevant to Hitler's

D

management of military matters. Like Napoleon before him, he was making pictures. Every 'fact', every 'truth' had to be fitted into this special picture of his own invention. 'When I use a word,' observed Humpty Dumpty, 'it means exactly what I want it to mean, neither more nor less.' And in the Humpty Dumpty world of Führer HQ, every military circumstance and condition meant only what Hitler wanted it to mean. So he was able to declare on 9 January, the same day that Guderian pleaded with him to adjust deployment and to send reinforcements, that since the Wehrmacht possessed 3,000 tanks and assault guns in the East and since the Red Army did not possess the necesary three-fold superiority required for a breakthrough, there would be, could be, no breakthrough. Leaving aside the distortion of numbers itself, such reasoning ignored completely the Russians' freedom of choice as to where they positioned their resources and what they did with them. Three days later, one or two more unpalatable facts were to make themselves known as Konev's Army Group swept across the frozen wastes of Southern Poland and sent Guderian's house of cards crashing down.

It was the greatest offensive of the war and it had no less than the end of the war as its strategic objective – a 45-day campaign to cross the Oder, seize Berlin and motor on to the Elbe. The broad plan made by the *Stavka** was in two phases – the first to advance from the Vistula to the Oder, the second on from the Oder. The two most important *fronts* were, of course, Konev's and Zhukov's with Rokossovsky and Petrov's respectively north and south playing subsidiary, flanking roles. The first objective – advance to the Oder – was rapidly achieved. The second took longer. The offensive actually began on 12 January when Konev's 1st Ukrainian *front* broke out of their Baranow bridgehead, while two days later Zhukov attacked from both the Magnuszew and Pulawy areas. Still further north Rokossovsky struck through the line of the Narew and drove towards the Gulf of Danzig, and Cherniakovsky smashed through the East Prussia defences towards Königsberg. Everywhere the Russians achieved clear breakthroughs. Static defences, inadequate in size and depth, and supported by insufficient mobile reserves, simply could not withstand the weight and speed plus the sheer depth and width of the Russian attack. In three weeks the Red Army had transformed the whole strategic situation in the East. By 4 February Zhukov had reached Küstrin, less than 50 miles from Berlin itself, Konev was at Breslau. Memel, Courland and the German divi-

Stavka, literally General Military Headquarters, i.e. Soviet Supreme Command.

sions in East Prussia, 25 in all, were cut off. The closing in was becoming close indeed.

Meanwhile what was Hitler up to? He had moved from *Eagle's Nest* back to Berlin on 16 January. The last Führer HQ was at last occupied for the last battle. On the same day he replaced Harpe, commanding Army Group A, by Schörner, and he cancelled Guderian's directive that Warsaw might be evacuated. When Warsaw fell on 17 January, Hitler once more flew into a rage, and conducted a fruitless campaign of revenge against Guderian and his staff. While Hitler was fulminating about the loss of Warsaw, German troops mounted an attack in Hungary in order to try and relieve Budapest. They reached the Danube, but the Russians reached Budapest. So obsessed did Hitler become with Budapest that some weeks later he sent off the 6th SS Panzer Army on a wild goose chase in Hungary instead of using it in the vital central sector. It was not only a side-show as far as space went. It wasted the other precious commodity – time. 'There could be no question', wrote Guderian, 'of launching the proposed offensive before early March. And how was Berlin to manage until then?' By 27 January 'the Russian tidal wave', as Guderian put it, 'was rapidly assuming the proportions of a complete disaster'. Everywhere the German armies were either being pulled back still further, being outflanked and captured, or simply being cut off. The Reichsführer, Himmler, was put in command of what was now called Army Group Vistula which was fighting between the Oder and the Vistula, although in view of the nearness of the Russians to the former, its name might more justly have been Army Group Oder. At his conference in the Bunker, Hitler concentrated on trivial detail at enormous length, and even permitted himself to be persuaded by Göring that in view of the Russian advances which must be thoroughly unwelcome to the Western Allies, they would any day be getting a telegram from them. In other words the nearer the Russians got to Berlin, the more ready would the Western Powers be to split with their Russian allies and make a compromise peace in order to keep Europe out of Communist hands.

How differently in fact were the minds of Churchill and Roosevelt moving. That there was disagreement between the Allies was clear enough, but it was not of the sort that Hitler and Göring imagined. It was the old question of their own strategy in the West which was causing so much concern. In spite of Eisenhower's knowing by the end of the first week in January that the Russians were shortly to embark on a great offensive, there was by no means unanimity of view between the British and the Americans either as to what should be done or how it should be done. On 10 January 1945 the Combined Chiefs of Staff had asked Eisenhower what his plans were. His reply ten days later made it plain that his strategy was dominated by the Rhine : getting to it, getting over it, advancing into Germany – and destroying all German forces encountered in the process. While holding to the view that the main attack should if possible be made north of the Ruhr, the Supreme Commander reserved the right to switch his main effort from north to south, that is the Frankfurt-Kassel axis. Yet when the plan was actually spelled out, it seemed clear that in fact Eisenhower intended to continue with an attack on two main axes, that is persist in what had always been and was to continue to be his idea for the whole Overlord Campaign – a broad front advance. The essential features of the plan were :

a. To carry out a series of operations North of the Moselle immediately with a view to destroying the enemy and closing the Rhine North of Düsseldorf.
b. After closing the Rhine in the North to direct our main effort to the destruction of all enemy forces remaining West of the Rhine.
c. To seize bridgeheads over the Rhine in the North and in the South.
d. To deploy East of the Rhine and North of the Ruhr the maximum number of divisions which can be maintained (estimated at some 35* divisions).
e. To deploy East of the Rhine, on the axis Frankfurt-Kassel, such forces, if adequate, as may be available after providing 35 divisions for the North and essential security elsewhere. The task of this force will be to draw enemy forces away from the North by capturing Frankfurt and advancing on Kassel.

If ever there were a general to whom the word Fabian really did apply – as opposed to Wellington to whom it did not – it was Eisenhower. Not surprisingly, the British Chiefs of Staff did not agree with this Fabian policy. They wanted all resources available to be concentrated in one thrust with the necessary reserve strength to maintain momentum. Only those forces which could not be employed in the main thrust should be considered for use in a subsidiary one, and this subsidiary advance should not be exploited unless it progressed at the same

---

*A puny total if we think of Stalin's 180 divisions, albeit smaller ones, earmarked for his central offensive.

time as the main one foundered. While accepting that the North was the place to go for, the British Chiefs of Staff reverted to Montgomery's old idea that there should be one Land Force Commander in charge of all forces committed to the main thrust. The Americans were as quick to record both their rejection of the British plan and their endorsement of Eisenhower's. Thus on the eve of discussions at Malta, between Churchill, Roosevelt and their Chiefs of Staff there appeared to be a major clash of opinion. Yet as the two great men were about to visit the third,* Stalin, it was peculiarly necessary that they themselves should be in accord. We shall see later how they resolved their differences at the *Argonaut* conference.

Before we do, however, it is perhaps important to emphasize that the *Argonaut* conference was concerned not so much with the grand strategy for winning the war (the die was more or less cast, although the preliminaries at Malta between the British and Americans were crucial), as with how to coordinate the efforts of the Western Allies and the Russians both to finish off Germany militarily and then to divide and administer their defeated enemy. The conference was thus of especial moment in relation to the prevailing and future situation of Berlin. What then was the military situation in relation to Berlin which held good at the beginning of February 1945? Chester Wilmot's point that Hitler courted defeat on the Vistula in the hope of gaining victory on the Meuse and recovery on the Danube sums it up as concisely as may be.

By 4 February 1945, the day that Churchill first saw Stalin at Yalta, the great Russian offensive had more or less come to a halt, although it had made prodigious strides. In the north Bagramyan had reached the Baltic, cutting off Courland and Memel; Cherniakovsky had overrun East Prussia; Rokossovsky was threatening Danzig; Zhukov had got to

---

*Sir Isaiah Berlin's comment on the big three – and other leading figures of the war – is worth recalling: 'Perhaps there is one respect in which the Second World War did outshine its predecessor: the leaders of the nations involved in it were, with the significant exception of France, men of greater stature, psychologically more interesting, than their prototypes. It would hardly be disputed that Stalin is a more fascinating figure than the Czar Nicholas II; Hitler more arresting than the Kaiser; Mussolini than Victor Emmanuel; and, memorable as they were, President Wilson and Lloyd George yield in the attribute of sheer historical magnitude to Franklin Roosevelt and Winston Churchill.' Only the last named, of course, was a war lord in both. Of these big three, however, with Churchill's loss of office and Roosevelt's death, Stalin alone remained as a constant factor in the cold war after 1945.

the Oder at Küstrin and Frankfurt, both less than 50 miles from Berlin; Konev too was on the Oder, indeed had bridgeheads over it and was but 120 miles from Prague; further south Malinovsky with a firm grip on Budapest was only 80 miles from Vienna. There was little doubt as to which armies were going to reach the great capitals of Eastern Europe first. How different were prospects on the Western front on that same day, 4 February. It was true that Hitler's Ardennes offensive had been defeated. But its defeat had not been accompanied by any giant and sweeping advances such as the Red Army had enjoyed. The American, British and French armies were still slogging their way slowly forward against skilful and determined defences. They had not even closed up to the Rhine and the Siegfried line along its full length. The reason for this great discrepancy between the fortunes of East and West was clear. Hitler *had* sought victory on the Meuse. Having after many months of patient planning, assembly of troops and weapons, indulgence in chimerical schemes of reviving the sort of miracles which had hauled the great Frederick from a strategic morass, and exhortations to his long-suffering commanders – after, to the amazement of many who had thought it impossible, creating a power-ful strategic reserve which contained no fewer than seven panzer divi-sions, Hitler had expended it in a gamble which had amongst others three important consequences. It had written off the strategic reserve, it had guaranteed the Red Army's success in the East, it had made certain that from that time forth the defence of Germany would roughly be what Hitler condemned as the operational ideas of all his generals – withdrawal to the next position until there were no more positions to withdraw to. What is more it had despatched Churchill and Roosevelt to Yalta with a disagreeable dearth of aces in their hands.

On 4 February then for the Western armies even though the Ameri-cans did at last capture some of the Ruhr dams (an operation which us v Corps had been engaged on more than six weeks earlier when the Ardennes attack started) Berlin was still far away. The Anglo-us forces were no more than getting ready to fulfil the first of Eisenhower's three broad requirements – to clear the Rhineland. Indeed as Chester Wilmot put it 'they were no nearer Berlin than they had been in September 1944, or for that matter in September 1939'. At this point the whole question of who was to have Berlin must have seemed academic even to the most sanguine of military men. Yet a swing of the scales was not to be long in making itself felt. It was the Red Army which was to get itself bogged down and it was the Western armies which within a little month were to get moving.*

On 1 February 1945, Himmler, the Reichsführer and Commander, Army Group Vistula (whose boundary ran roughly from the Vistula Delta to Kulm and thence via Küstrin to Glogan, and which therefore protected the approaches to Berlin) wrote to Guderian, still at this time Army Chief of Staff about the premature and beneficial thaw at the end of January. Himmler, like Hitler himself, was a believer in miracles. 'I know,' he confided to a friend as late as April 1945, 'that I am generally regarded as a heedless pagan, but in the depths of my heart I am a believer in God and Providence. In the course of the last year I have learned to believe in miracles again. The Führer's escape on 20 July was a miracle; and a second I have experienced in my own life, this very spring.' The second one was this thaw on the Oder just when the Red Army was about to advance across the ice. To Guderian, Himmler described the thaw as a gift of fate. God had not forgotten the courageous German people. Both on the fronts of Army Group Vistula and Army Group Centre (formerly A) commanded by Schörner the foundations of a defensive position were taking shape. Schörner, competent, sometimes easy going in appearance but hard enough underneath, a Hitler man through and through, sent a signal to his Commander-in-Chief on that same day, 4 February: 'My Führer! I can report that the first onslaught of the great Russian offensive has been substantially intercepted. The front is still under pressure in many places, but in others we are making local counter-attacks.'

The Russian offensive may have been temporarily halted – it did not alter the fact that the impact of the Red Army on German soil was profound. When the Russian soldiers entered Silesia and Pomerania, they entered a world hitherto unknown to them. Prosperous, peaceful, and until this time virtually unmarked by war, except that Speer had established new industries there, well away from the effects of Anglo/American bombs, it was about to be scourged. 'Through this countryside,' noted Alan Clark, 'the Soviet columns literally blazed their trail. Shops, houses, farms were plundered and set alight. Civilians were shot down casually for the possessions they carried with them; it was common for a man to be murdered for his wrist watch. The Russians soon discovered that the inhabitants were hiding their womenfolk in

---

*It is worth recalling that in spite of all the dismay and disruption caused by the Ardennes offensive, Montgomery's crossing of the Rhine was not badly delayed. Before the offensive began he had planned it for mid-March. It took place on 24 March.

the cellars of their houses and adopted the practice of setting fire to
buildings they suspected were being used for this purpose. An incendi-
ary shell from a T34 proved the quickest way to assemble the occupants
for scrutiny.' But, Alan Clark goes on to point out, all this brutality and
destruction was capricious, not as it was in reverse when the SS had
followed the invading Army Groups into White Russia – a matter of
deliberate extermination of Slav *Untermenschen*. The Russian soldier
was rough and tough, indifferent to life and death, and had been
taught to hate his enemy. No wonder he had little thought in robbing
and killing, burning and looting. It was all part of the game, the spoils
of conquest and in some cases the satisfaction of revenge. '*Wir haben
viel kaputt gemacht*,' observed to me long after the war a land-owning
aristocrat of Westphalia who had accompanied the Wehrmacht deep
into the Soviet Union, '*aber sie waren keine Menschen*; *sie waren
Tiere*.'* The animals were now behaving themselves according to their
own lights. In choosing between the respective ideas of Kant who
recommended that hostilities between states at war should never take
such a form as to render subsequent mutual confidence impossible and
of Nietzsche who maintained that injury, violation, exploitation,
annihilation could not be wrong *per se* for life presupposed them –
there was little doubt to which direction Hitler's *Weltanschauung*
inclined. Not for him the great Churchillian ideas which could couple
victory and magnanimity.

All this aside the great Russian advance would give Stalin a powerful hand to play – both psychologically and strategically – when it
came to talking with his colleagues about how to finish off the war and
arranging the peace. We have seen that there was already disagreement between the British and American Chiefs of Staff as to the exact
conduct of military affairs on the Western front and this made
Churchill particularly anxious that there should be preliminary discussions between these staffs and if possible between himself and Roosevelt
before meeting the Russians at Yalta. The short talks between the
President and the Prime Minister on board USS *Quincy* immediately
before flying to Russia were harmonious. Discussions between the
Allied Chiefs of Staff were not harmonious. It will be remembered that
the principal points of discord were – what thrusts should be made into
Germany and how would they be commanded. These questions were
discussed in Malta by the Combined Chiefs of Staff from 30 January to
1 February.

The question of command – probably the less important of the two,

*'We did a lot of damage, but they weren't people; they were animals.'

for whatever else might be said about it, Eisenhower's conduct of
Overlord had brought the Allies from the shores of England to the
frontiers of Germany in less than six months – paradoxically enough
engendered the more heat. The real disagreement, of course, although
it was not the way in which the British deployed their arguments, was
not *how* command of the land battle was to be exercised, but *by whom*.
Not to put too fine a point on it, the British were mistrustful of both
Eisenhower's real understanding of the strategic issues and his determination to carry out in practice what he might agree to in theory.
There was, it seemed to them, only one way in which to ensure that the
plan was sound and properly carried out, and that was to have a
British plan and a British land commander operating under Eisenhower. Not unexpectedly the United States Joint Chiefs of Staff, who
had long been rejecting Montgomery's wish to return to the early
arrangements of *Overlord* when he had enjoyed complete control of
the land battle, resisted firmly. It was not only that they disagreed
about the command arguments. They were anxious to avoid circumstances in which the British, by having too strong a hand in command,
would call the strategic tune to the extent where the plans executed
would be contrary to those of the Supreme Commander endorsed by
themselves. Although the Joint Chiefs of Staff had their way over the
question of command, the mere fact of there being an acrimonious
discussion here did not ease the discussion about the strategy itself.

Yet agreement to compromise on strategy or rather to elucidate it
was fairly quickly reached. Field Marshal Sir Alan Brooke summarized
the British objection which was that having two thrusts against the
expected opposing strengths precluded the possibility of either one
being decisive. The American view was that it would be wrong to stake
all on a single thrust particularly on so narrow a front. The advance
further south should not be regarded as being in competition with the
northern one, but essentially complementary, to aid the northern one
by drawing off enemy strength and to be an alternative if necessary. It
would take no strength from the principal attack whose total of 36*
divisions (plus 10 in reserve) was determined and limited by communications. Thus the employment of about 12 divisions in the south, divisions which could not be used in the north, might turn the scales for the
main thrust. In the end the only thing that needed changing – as so
often when controversy over policy resolves itself into disagreement
about semantics – was the wording of the Supreme Commander's
intentions. A new version removed reference to the possible need for

*Rather than 35 mentioned in Eisenhower's plan.

using either or both of the two approaches and also to the need to close
the Rhine throughout its length as a preliminary to further advance.
Eisenhower accepted his revised plan and assured the Combined Chiefs
of Staff that he would seize the Rhine crossings in the North immediately it became feasible and without waiting to close up to the river
everywhere. Furthermore the northern crossing would be done in
maximum strength and absolute determination as soon as the forces
were ready and security elsewhere assured. Both parties expressed
themselves satisfied with the Malta talks. But whereas the Americans
reported that the Combined Chiefs of Staff had endorsed Eisenhower's
views, the British maintained that Eisenhower's intentions conformed
with the Prime Minister's and his military advisers' wishes. There was,
however, one curious omission in the Supreme Commander's instructions. There was no mention of Berlin.

   This was all the more strange because London's first reaction to
Eisenhower's plans had been to stress that the primary object of the
whole thing was to mount operations aimed at the heart of Germany.
The British had always supposed that the northern thrust apart from
capturing the Ruhr was the right one because it represented the
shortest road to the German capital. Indeed in May 1944 even before
Overlord started, the Western Armies' goal had been defined as Berlin.
What had happened in Malta – agreement to concentrate on the
northern thrust – seemed to confirm the British point of view. Yet even
as late as the time when his armies were deploying from the eastern
bank of the Rhine, Eisenhower had still not decided the pattern of his
advance into the heart of Germany. Stranger still, no directive from the
Combined Chiefs of Staff laid it down. Herein lay the seeds of further
disagreement and further strategic dithering. Eisenhower referred at
this time to his intention to link up at Kassel the primary and secondary attacks and then thrust east from there. But where to had not been
specified.

   The opposing Supreme Commander had less choice in the matter.
His gamble in the West had failed. His conduct of the war in the East
was so eccentric and so tactically unsound that he had left weakest the
very area where the threat was greatest. He had frittered away on the
Meuse and the Danube what he was about to need so desperately on
the Rhine and the Oder. No wonder Guderian had asked Ribbentrop
in the last week of January how he would feel if in three or four weeks'
time the Russians were at the gates of Berlin. When Ribbentrop protested and asked if that was really possible, Guderian replied that as a
result of the Third Reich's leadership it was certain. Guderian had

been trying to persuade Ribbentrop to go with him to Hitler and propose to the Führer that in view of the hopelessness of the military situation, they should seek an armistice in the West. Needless to say the footling and fearful Ribbentrop refused to contemplate so dangerous a course of action. As Guderian himself recorded in his memoirs – 'at that time the Western Powers were hardly in a mood to take part in any such negotiations, particularly since they had bound themselves by an agreement with the Russians only to deal with Germany collectively.' Nevertheless, he was convinced that it was necessary to try and induce Hitler to do so. Had he been allowed to listen to the deliberations of the three great men at Yalta, he might have been less sure.

4

YALTA

Mr Roosevelt was intrigued by the Russian Sphinx; Mr Churchill instinctively recoiled from its alien and to him unattractive attributes.

ISAIAH BERLIN

Melbourne once said that he wished he could be as cocksure about anything as Macaulay was about everything. The fact that Melbourne as Prime Minister behaved in so dilettante a fashion, urging inaction rather than taking firm steps, remaining full of doubt as to the need for this or that, lends weight to Pope's contention that the most positive men are the most credulous. Credulity and positivism played no small part in determining the outcome of Yalta. The credulity was largely Roosevelt's, the positivism Stalin's. Churchill's instinct steered an unwavering course between the two. These three men at Yalta set the stage for the closing scenes of the greatest conflict the world has ever known. Not only the men themselves deserve our attention but together with their widely divergent views of strategic priorities and the use of power comes the sort of relationship in which they stood to each other.

These relationships were inevitably much affected by the very different positions they held in their own countries in respect of their military forces. Roosevelt was at once President of the United States and Commander-in-Chief of his country's armed forces. If anything he concentrated on the latter task rather than the former. But he did so in the realms of broadest strategy and in the mistaken belief that his ideas would take a similar hold of those beyond the frontiers of the New World as they had taken of himself. He was more concerned with preventing Congress from interfering with the general conduct of the war than in ensuring that the decision-making machinery for its conduct was orderly, disciplined and economic. His whole concept of the post-war world was that the various peoples of it would have so much in common that the creation of a world order embracing freedom and prosperity would be a simple and almost automatic process. In his dealings with his subordinate commanders, he displayed an extraordinary mixture of eccentricity and inconsistency. He would not hesitate to overrule Marshall and Eisenhower in the – to the Allies – critical decision to land in North Africa in 1942, yet, by delegating command of the armies in Europe to Eisenhower, he exercised virtually no control at all over what the Supreme Commander did with them. In the judgment and handling of his major political colleagues he showed a prejudice, a naivety and a stubbornness astonishing in a figure so imaginative and empirical. He could not stand de Gaulle, and we find him writing to Churchill in April 1944 that he would under no circumstances invite the French leader to Washington. He somehow deceived himself that Stalin 'likes me better', and that he, Roosevelt, could 'handle' Stalin better than others. Only once in his judgment of war leaders did he come near to hitting the target accurately, and that was in his view of Churchill whom he admired, respected and liked. But then, of course, with Churchill he had been in almost daily contact by telegram or letter throughout the great conflict. And certain characteristics he shared absolutely with the Prime Minister. Both were confident of victory even in the darkest days, both sustained their people against all disappointments and delays, and both were never wholly trusted by those about them.

Distrust of Churchill – that is on the part of those concerned with conduct of the war – was occasioned not by the man, but by his methods. While never overruling the Chiefs of Staff, he did his best by cajolery, bullying, rhetoric, second opinions and sheer physical endurance to wear them down. His judgment of commanders in the field was coloured often more by sympathy with personality than by analysis of merit.* It is, for example, a permanent puzzle that Wavell, with so many qualities in common such as vision, simplicity, boldness, historical imagination, deep love of literature and an inner, sustaining strength of purpose was never on the same 'net' as Churchill. He made the mistake of being too silent. Just as George II, when informed that Wolfe was mad, expressed the wish that he would bite some other generals, so we might suggest that Wavell's silence could have been distributed to some of his fellows with benefit to all. Churchill's position as His Majesty's First Minister and Minister of Defence was such that in the making of strategy – subject always to endorsement by the Chiefs of Staff – he had almost supreme power. The only condition which tempered his

---

*Even the merit of being right when he, Churchill, was wrong. But this singular occurrence predictably contained no merit in Churchill's eyes.

power was his survival as head of the Government. He always maintained that he liked the Russians, but was the first to warn against the threat they posed to a free and recovering Europe. He defined the difficulty of dealing with them as the uncertainty of their reactions. 'One strokes the nose of the alligator and the ensuing gurgle may be a purr of affection, a grunt of stimulated appetite, or a snarl of enraged animosity. One cannot tell.' His astonishing strategic vision and boldness in executing it was at times utterly contradicted by crackpot ideas about weapons or campaigns. His insistence on 'succouring' Greece in 1941 was a romantic gesture which simply ensured the prolongation of the North African war. His refusal to understand the realities of the Japanese threat to Great Britain's Eastern empire was equalled only by his notion that the United States would ever support a major attack in the Balkans or in Norway when their eyes were fixed firmly on the central group of the Wehrmacht's armies in France and Germany. But his declaration to the French in 1940 that 'we shall fight on for ever and ever and ever' no matter what they might do was not merely magnificent in its own right. It was symbolic of the man himself.

If one needed a thumbnail portrait of the third member of this remarkable triumvirate, a summing up of the motif of Generalissimo Joseph Stalin, it is perhaps best provided by Aleksandr Solzhenitsyn: 'Neither dismissal, nor ostracism, nor the insane asylum, nor life imprisonment, nor exile seemed to him sufficient punishment for a person he recognized as dangerous. *Death* was the only reliable means of settling accounts in full. And when his lower lids squinted, the sentence which shone in his eyes was always *death*.' It was as well for Stalin and as well for the Soviet Union that he never regarded Zhukov as too dangerous, for if ever there were an architect of victory before and after Yalta, it was Marshal Zhukov, who rather surprisingly recalled in his memoirs that Stalin 'won the heart of everyone he talked with'. Either won it, we might add, or persuaded it to study a long silence.

According to Zhukov, Stalin's conduct of the war was characterized by overall control of his country's military resources, a firm grip on general strategy, considerable dependence on the *military* view of his principal commanders, no hesitation in interfering with the detail of operations and sometimes an extraordinarily childish tendency to cut Zhukov down to size. In mid-November 1941 before the desperate battle for Moscow developed, Stalin insisted against Zhukov's advice on mounting a spoiling counter-attack. When he ordered two specific blows to be launched at the German forces assembling for the drive on

Moscow, and Zhukov enquired what formations were to be employed for *he* had none to spare, Stalin was specific as to which divisions should be made available. On Zhukov's objecting that these reserves could not be used for it would mean that there would be nothing to reinforce his armies with when the German attack began, Stalin drily observed that Zhukov already had six armies in his *front*. 'Isn't that enough?' When Zhukov once more tried to point out that some depth was required, he was curtly told that the whole matter of mounting a counter-strike had already been decided and that Zhukov was to let him have the plan that evening.

In the event the two attacks, German and Russian, were more or less simultaneous. Moscow, as we know, was held. During the critical phases of the battle, Zhukov did not hesitate to ask for reserve armies and Stalin did not hesitate to provide them. Nor did Stalin hesitate to overrule Zhukov time after time. Like Churchill, he rather enjoyed 'nudging the military'. Stalin had something in common with Hitler too in that he would issue his directives as Supreme Commander-in-Chief, and no discussion could move him. Having heard all sorts of objections to his plans and having reiterated his intentions to stick in every detail to his ideas, he would bring conferences to a close with simple statements like : 'So be it; on that we shall end the discussions.' Some of the exchanges between Zhukov and Stalin put one in mind of comparable dealings between Hitler and his field commanders. When Stalin ordered First Shock Army to be withdrawn into *Stavka* reserve in January 1942, and Zhukov protested, he was simply told that it was the Supreme Commander-in-Chief's order, which like the Führer's order was unalterable. Direct communication with the Generalissimo himself simply resulted in Stalin's giving a direct order and hanging up the telephone when Zhukov still remonstrated. Even Khrushchev, never one to hesitate to put in his oar if he thought military mistakes were being made, had to put up with : 'Comrade Stalin has made up his mind and that's all there is to it.'

There was in short no doubt as to who was wielding supreme command, a point heavily reinforced by Stalin's directive during the battle for Stalingrad. But it would be wrong to lose sight of the point that the *Stavka* as a whole both conceived grand Soviet strategy and directed its execution. Stalin may have been the most powerful and influential figure in the *Stavka*; Zhukov was certainly its most professionally sound member. The two may not have always seen eye to eye, there may have been lack of mutual confidence at times, even open hostility, yet Stalin was not blind to the proof of who was his most successful general. When the plans were being made for the assault on Germany, the great January battles which we have already discussed, Stalin announced that Berlin would be taken by the armies of Zhukov's 1st Belorussian *front*. In other words the great plum and prize was to be reserved for Zhukov. And the decision, arbitrary and absolute, in no way based on military reasoning, was Stalin's alone. It is somehow difficult to reconcile the mild 'Uncle Joe' referred to so tolerantly, even affectionately, by Churchill and Roosevelt in their exchange of telegrams with the 'sullen paranoiac who destroyed more of his fellow countrymen than all of the Tsars put together,' Yet such was the man with whom Churchill and Roosevelt were to deal in finishing off the war and organizing the peace. What were the real issues at Yalta and what were the separate aims of these three men?

'The whole shape and structure of post-war Europe', wrote Churchill, 'clamoured for review. When the Nazis were beaten how was Germany to be treated? What aid could we expect from the Soviet Union in the final overthrow of Japan? And once military aims were achieved what measures and what organization could the three great Allies provide for the future peace and good government of the world?' There was also the question of Poland. Unsatisfactory exchanges between Roosevelt and Stalin on this matter resulted in the Russian leader's issuing an invitation to his two Allies. Roosevelt was as convinced as Churchill that only a meeting of the Big Three could resolve both individual problems, the general war situation and the ways in which to move towards peace. But the three leaders were in very different situations as to what they wanted and what they could offer.

The big military issues were first, how the Western Allies would set about defeating Germany (this as we have seen was decided at Malta – before the Three met), secondly, how the operations for Germany's defeat should be coordinated with the Russians, and thirdly, how all three would divide their responsibilities for the countries which had come under their control. The third of these would obviously depend largely on the second, and the second would – apart from Russia's own hand in the affair – depend on the first. In short when would the war end and where would the line-up of the Allied armies be? The various British estimates of the date for the end of the war in Europe made between June 1944 and its end are remarkable not for discrepancy, but for consistency. Nine days after D-day in Normandy, the Prime Minister laid down that plans must be based on the war's continuing for a further year. Apart from one or two slightly more optimistic guesses, and one extremely pessimistic one made by the War Cabinet on 12

Eisenhower, Montgomery and Bradley

Churchill, Stalin and Roosevelt

January 1945, which foresaw a possibility of war not ending before 31 December 1945, all agencies concerned – the Joint Planning Staff, the War Cabinet, the Combined Chiefs of Staff, the Prime Minister himself – stuck more or less to midway through 1945. In spite of this astonishing accuracy none of them made it plain or even hinted that the city of Berlin was the key to the whole thing, the supreme military objective, the one place which had to be taken before the Third Reich would submit – not because of any overriding strategic importance that the capital *per se* had, but simply that it contained the one man who kept the whole machinery of the Wehrmacht ticking over, no matter how tenuous his actual control, the one man whose death, capture or capitulation was indispensable to the end of hostilities – the Führer himself. Had this point figured more largely in the first of the principal issues – the Western Allies' strategy finally to encompass the defeat of Germany – those same Allies might have had less difficulty in resolving the problems which arose from the other two.

The trouble was that at this time the Allies were not in a position to think big about Berlin. Almost the whole of Eastern Europe was in Russian hands. In any case Roosevelt was not interested in Berlin, nor in exactly *how* the war ended. What he wanted was that the European war should end quickly and that the Soviet Union would then lend her aid to finish off Japan. Stalin was obviously in a position to do something to help with these two objectives since he had at his disposal the means both further to hammer the Germans and also to bring pressure to bear on Japan. Churchill, who was much more concerned about the growing Soviet threat both to the Western position in post-war Europe as a whole, the deteriorating position of Poland, and the growing claims over German territory and German reparations which the Soviet Union was sponsoring, was not in a position to help in the same way. Britain had shot its military bolt. A rather absurd situation thus developed in that Roosevelt, whose real interests and proper aims even though he may not have realized it, were closely aligned with those of Churchill, having gained the assurance he sought from Stalin, lent little or no support to Churchill as the Prime Minister tried to get his apprehensions dissolved.

The essential difference of the various attitudes of these three men again reflected both their character and their principles. President Roosevelt believed in the United Nations. Generalissimo Stalin believed in the power of the Red Army and all the associated instruments of terror which territory occupied by the Red Army would be subject to. Mr. Churchill believed in lessons of the past, in his own strategic and historical instinct, in moderation and balance of power. It was not to be expected that they would agree about all the great issues which were scrutinized at Yalta. The tragedy which eroded so much of the triumphs to come, was that Churchill completely failed to convince Roosevelt that Stalin had not fundamentally changed from his own judgment of the Russian leader made several years earlier as 'a crafty, callous and ill-informed giant'.

Stalin's ignorance was notable in both its nature and its range. A review of *The Semblance of Peace** made clear that this ignorance was not modified by victory :

> He was ignorant of Western Europe : he did not even know which three countries formed Benelux. He was ignorant of the Balkans : the significance of the Macedonian problem in the Greek civil war seems to have escaped him entirely. He was ignorant of the United States, to the extent of believing in 1948 that Henry Wallace would be the next president. He was ignorant even of China, as witness his mis-calculation of the chances of Mao Tse-tung against Chiang Kai-shek. His sole concern from first to last was the security of the Russian state, which he identified with himself.

It was concern for the Soviet Union's security which most influenced him at Yalta, and one matter of overriding importance to him in this respect, which in turn would influence the battle for Berlin, was the planned dismemberment of Germany. Agreement in principle as to the need to dismember Germany was more easily reached than agreement as to practical methods of doing so. Reference to the former was made in the Instrument of Surrender by the inclusion of an article which laid down that the three Powers would possess supreme author-ity with respect to Germany, and that in the exercise of this authority they would take those steps necessary to ensure future peace and security, including 'the complete disarmament, demilitarization and the dismemberment of Germany'. Resolution of the latter was left to a special committee. But one further point of principle, which had great influence on putting the whole thing into practice was agreed at Yalta

---

*By John Wheeler-Bennett and Anthony Nicholls, London, 1972. (*TLS* 22 September 1972).

†Germany was not of course dismembered. By the time the Allies conferred at Potsdam the policy of dismemberment had been dropped. While no central German government was to be established, it was clear that dismemberment and reparations were incompatible. Not surprisingly West and East chose reparations

– that is the question of giving a zone of occupation to the French. Churchill was all the more anxious that this should be done because of Roosevelt's statement that United States troops would probably stay in Europe for no more than two years. In discussion of this question Stalin and Roosevelt did not show that magnanimity which the Prime Minister had always advocated. Stalin, perhaps forgetting his own dealings with the Führer immediately before and during the first two years of war, complained that the French had not stood firm against the enemy, had indeed opened the gates to them. Roosevelt was inclined to allow the French a zone without a voice in the Control Commission – an absurd contradiction. He later was persuaded to concede that the French would perhaps be less trouble in the Control Commission than outside it. When Roosevelt withdrew his opposition, so did Stalin, and Churchill in this instance had his way.

Of more immediate pertinence to our story here is the military aspect of these decisions, that is how the Western Allies should coordinate their military plans with the Russians for the last phase of the war in Europe, and how to arrange that when in fact the war was over the areas then occupied by the armies of the Allied powers should be so adjusted that they conformed with what had already been agreed about the future administration of Germany. One of the trickiest problems of liaison lay in the selection of 'bomb lines' defining where the respective bomber forces could and could not operate. The closer the Western Armies and the Red Army approached each other, the trickier the problem became. The different methods of operation between the Soviet land forces on the one hand and the Anglo-US forces on the other did not ease matters. The Anglo-US position was clearly laid down in a Combined Chiefs of Staff message sent to Moscow some two weeks before the Yalta conference began. The main difference between the two sides, as might have been expected, was that, whereas the Allies were content to delegate authority in such matters to their theatre commanders, the Russians plumped for centralized control in Moscow. The Combined Chiefs of Staff message recognized 'the Soviet right to establish bomb lines to protect their own forces in the Balkans and in Eastern Europe' subject to several conditions. The Soviet Command must accept the Western definition* of a

---

* The essential points were that between the bomb line (an imaginary and easily recognizable line on the ground such as a town, river or railway) and the forward troops, air attacks on ground targets were prohibited. The line was close enough to allow attacks on tactical or strategic targets which would assist troops to advance. It did not restrict the *movement* of friendly aircraft.

bomb line. Allied aircraft must have the right to fly over areas occupied
by Soviet forces. Short of agreement on these points the Soviet Union
would have to share responsibility for 'mistakes'. Meanwhile the appropriate Allied commanders were authorized to adjust bomb lines both
south and north of the latitude of Vienna while ensuring that all
interested parties, including the Red Army Staff, were kept informed.
And it was this general sort of rule which prevailed. Such were the
difficulties of liaison on air matters.

Liaison on the ground was no less hard. However anxious the British
and Americans may have been to establish effective liaison between the
Army Commanders on the Eastern and Western fronts, the Russian
view at Yalta was that 'at the present time no tactical cooperation was
required between Allied and Russian ground forces'. In reality the time
was fast approaching when some sort of cooperation or at least understanding on one another's intentions would be indispensable if uninten-
tional clashes were to be avoided. Yet when Field-Marshal Sir Alan
Brooke and General George Marshall tried to get satisfaction on this
point from General Antonev, in relation to operations in March and
April, the Russian general merely replied that they would continue
their offensive in the East as long as the weather allowed and to the
limit of their capacity. That these operations should be understood by
all was peculiarly relevant to the proposed post-war zones of occupation in Austria and Germany and areas of responsibility in south east
Europe. As to the last of these areas Churchill's half sheet of paper
pushed across the table to Stalin with its percentages on it is well
known. 'Let us settle our affairs in the Balkans,' he had said by way of
introducing the subject. 'Your armies are in Rumania and Bulgaria.
We have interest, missions, and agents there. Don't let us get at cross
purposes in small ways. So far as Britain and Russia are concerned,
how would it do for you to have ninety per cent predominance in
Rumania, for us to have ninety per cent of the say in Greece, and go
fifty-fifty about Yugoslavia?' Stalin agreed. So, more or less, it transpired and so, as far as influence is concerned, it was more or less
endorsed.

The Austrian zones of occupation which had been under consideration since August 1944 were not discussed at Yalta, but by April 1945
were settled. The British were to have Carinthia and Styria; the
Americans would occupy Upper Austria, Salzburg and Tyrol-
Vorarlberg; Lower Austria would be for the Russians. The German
zones of occupation, too, had long been under discussion. The *Octagon*
conference in Quebec between the British and Americans had proposed

three zones – British north-east, Americans south-west (with a special enclave at Bremen plus appropriate communication rights to their zone), Russians east. Berlin would have three sectors each occupied by the troops of its own nation. The three Commandants would administer the city as an 'Inter-Allied Governing Authority'. All these arrangements for Germany would begin after her surrender. Although these proposals were endorsed at Yalta, they were, as noted already, altered by the allocation of a zone to the French. This zone was to be formed from the British and American zones.

All in all therefore the decisions taken at Yalta were concerned less with how to end the war than with what to do when the war was over. Diplomacy rather than strategy ruled the roost. It was the very powerful strategic position of the Soviet Union which enabled Stalin to stick to his principal objectives. Yet what in fact had the British and Americans given up? Perhaps only one thing – the future of Poland, the very country whose threatened freedom had started the war itself, in that it was the Soviet Union who would dominate the future Polish government. Poland was so firmly in Russian hands that short of allying themselves with the Third Reich and taking on the Soviet Union, there was probably little that the Western Allies could have done to alter Poland's fate.

What however would be the fate of Germany? Would she be occupied largely by the Russians who had already conquered East Prussia and were across the Oder within striking distance of Berlin? What chance had the Western armies even of occupying the zones allotted to them when they were not even across the Rhine? How in short would the decisions taken at Yalta affect military affairs and how would military affairs give reality to or utterly contradict decisions taken at Yalta? How above all would what had been decided at Yalta affect the final battles for Germany and for Berlin itself?

One decision, of course, whose influence was important was the confirmation by the Three of the policy of 'Unconditional Surrender'. It was not so much a question that without this policy the Third Reich would have collapsed more quickly. Professor Trevor-Roper has recorded his views here and they are convincing. 'It is sometimes said', he wrote :

that the Allied insistence on unconditional surrender frightened the Germans into continued obedience; but if this implies that they would otherwise have revolted, I do not think it is true. Of those Germans who preferred the rule of the Nazis to unconditional surrender, how many would have been inspired to rebellion by an Allied assurance of moderation? ... the Army leaders might perhaps have been ready to bargain; but conditions which included the destruction of the German Army would have seemed no conditions to them. ... As for the democratic opposition, invented by virtuous journalists, it is a creature as fabulous as the centaur and the hippogriff ... in time of war, bargains can only be struck with real political forces, not with whimpering shadows. ...

No, it is not the effect of the Allies' Unconditional Surrender policy on the Germans which must hold our attention when we examine the closing months of the war. It is its effect on the Allies themselves. Eisenhower's final plans were inhibited by a recurring lack of clear objectives and in the end he dealt directly with Stalin in agreeing that the mythological Alpine Redoubt was more important for the American armies than was the capital of the Third Reich.* Stalin himself when he suspected – wrongly – in March 1945 that the Western Allies were about to do a deal with General Wolff, Head of the SS in Italy, which would have enabled the Western armies to advance unopposed, allowed himself the luxury of some ill-advised accusatory telegrams to the other Two.

When Chester Wilmot called Yalta Stalin's greatest victory, he was thinking not so much of what was actually agreed by the Three at their conference, but the subsequent political consequences. It has since been pointed out that the occupation of Eastern Europe by the Russians could hardly be regarded as a political defeat by the Western Allies as they had no expectation of occupying it themselves. The Russians' part in defeating Germany had been more conclusive than any othe single country's. Without them there would have been no invasion of Normandy, and perhaps no invasion of Germany, although it may be supposed that military victory for the West was absolutely assured once the atomic bomb had been developed to the point of its being usable – always provided that the West would have been willing to use it in Europe – and that without the Russians as Allies, the West had not previously been defeated. One thing was certain – that the military occupation of Europe while the war still lasted was bound to affect political spheres of influence once it was over. How, if at all, were military plans for the final overrunning and defeat of Germany geared to the zones of occupation which had already been agreed, or would it

*'One can imagine the smile on the face of the bear when it was agreed that Berlin was not an important objective.' *Times Literary Supplement.*

rather be a question of the Western and Red armies simply forging on until they met somewhere between the Rhine and the Oder? The question of where exactly they would meet would depend not only on respective Western and Soviet plans but also on how what remained of the Wehrmacht was to be employed.

Before we consider that, it would be as well to remember that during the discussion or altercations at Yalta as to Germany's future, Churchill had made his position clear. He and Stalin were far more concerned with what happened to Germany than was Roosevelt. To the American President Germany was not a key question at all, it was simply a pawn in the bigger game of getting Russian aid in defeating Japan and Russian support in establishing the United Nations in the form he, Roosevelt, wanted. Stalin's *cri de coeur* (perhaps *cri de guerre* would be a better way to put it) on behalf of Poland, or rather on behalf of Russia in that a strong and large Poland, particularly one under his own control, would add to the Soviet Union's security, prompted him to the extraordinary statement that 'I would prefer the war to continue a little longer ... to give Poland compensation in the West at the expense of the Germans ... I am in favour of extending the Polish Western frontier to the Neisse River' – in other words giving Poland most of Silesia. Churchill's celebrated reply was to the effect that if the Polish goose were stuffed so full of German food, he might die of indigestion.

Yalta was conspicuous for great statements which bore little relation to reality. None however was so far removed from actuality as Hitler's comments about the conference :

> Those warmongers in Yalta must be denounced – so insulted and attacked that they will have no chance to make an offer to the German people. Under no circumstances must there be an offer. That gang only wants to separate the German people from their leadership. I've always said surrender is absolutely out of the question. History is not going to be repeated.

It is true that there was no surrender – not in the sense Hitler meant, and not in any case until after his death. Nor was history repeated. But all these fine words apart, Hitler was compelled to decide once more on the priorities of the Eastern and Western fronts. He had counter-attacked in the West and the attack had failed. He had forecast such dissension between the Western Allies and the Russians – particularly in view of the gigantic advances of the Red Army – that their alliance would fall apart and a telegram from the West would propose a separate peace. No telegram had come and the Three had reiterated their determination to 'destroy the last vestiges of Nazism and Fascism'. He had argued that the secret weapons – submarines, V rockets and jet aircraft – would at last turn the scales. None had materialized in the numbers required to do so. But the business of containing the armies which were pressing in on the Third Reich persisted, and decision as to what to do was urgent. Since the threat to Berlin was so close and substantial, and Hitler himself was in Berlin, it is not to be wondered at that he chose to reinforce the East. Having previously courted defeat on the Vistula in the hope of gaining decision on the Meuse, he was now to risk collapse on the Rhine in order to halt disintegration on the Oder. It was therefore going to be the turn of the Anglo-American armies to advance.

Hitler's decision to go on with the fight and on no account to surrender was almost certainly supported by the bulk of the German people. This was not only because the Red Army was in so much better a position – deployed on and even across the Oder – to surge across the Reich to destroy and plunder than were the Western Allies, the other side of the Siegfried line. It was also, astonishingly enough, because many of them still believed in the man. When Albert Speer visited the Western front on the Rhine in February 1945, the same month as Yalta, he discovered in talking to ordinary soldiers and workers that they still had faith in the Führer. 'They believed that he, and only he, both understood the working class from which he had risen, and the mystery of politics which had been concealed from the rest of the German race, and that he would therefore be able, as no one else, to work the miracle of their salvation from this forlorn predicament.'

Certainly to Hitler himself, the cause was not yet lost. He still kept hoping, like Mr Micawber, in spite of all the evidence against it, that something would turn up. If those German soldiers and workers who still believed in him could have known his real thoughts about them, their belief might have been less solid. Nothing had changed in the sentiments he had expressed while facing another crisis two years earlier when the game in Russia had begun to go badly wrong. 'As long as there is one strong-hearted man to hold up the banner, nothing has been lost. In this respect, I am ice-cold. If the German people are not prepared to give everything for the sake of their self-preservation, very well! Then let them disappear.' Sir Eyre Coote once made the point that political and strategic considerations must go hand in hand, and that failure to harmonize them led in turn either to political or military failure. We have seen many confirmations of this dictum. Guderian's plea to withdraw Army Group North from the Baltic States before it was cut off appeared on military grounds to be indisputable. Hitler's utter rejection of it was based wholly on political considerations. The terrible confusion which reigned as to what objectives to go for in Russia after the first fine careless rapture of galloping across the steppes, destroying or capturing everything in the Panzer-Schwerpunkte's paths, was due to absolute neglect of the need to harmonize the two considerations. The Anglo-French fiasco at Suez was a more recent instance. American frustration in Vietnam was a compelling reminder that the equation continues to hold good.

There had been times when Hitler not merely acknowledged its truth, but seized on its practice in such a way as to give a devastating illustration of the success which awaited conformation to the formula – witness only the *Anschluss* and Munich. Hitler had always tried to keep them hand in hand, but he had discovered that this was only possible while he held the cards, while the initiative remained in his hands. He still combined in his own person the supreme direction of both political and strategic affairs. He could still keep them in harmony if he so wished. But even if he did, was it not probable that far from having to choose *between* political or military defeat, he would, whatever he did, have to reconcile himself to both? This surely was the reflection which faced him as he settled down at the last of the Führer Headquarters in Berlin.

5

THREATS TO BERLIN

Berlin had become a second Carthage – and the final agony was still to come.

CORNELIUS RYAN

The battle *of* Berlin, rather than *for* it, had begun as early as August 1940, when the Royal Air Force bombed the city for the first time. It was perhaps not surprising that a man like Air Chief Marshal Sir Arthur Harris, believing as he did so passionately in the ability of Bomber Command to win the war off its own bat, convinced of the efficacy of a general area offensive, seeing only extremes and never the all but inevitable compromises of strategy, should have thought that the Battle of Berlin could be decisive. The Chief of the Air Staff, Sir Charles Portal, tended more to the selective target – oil or ball-bearings. 'While area bombing,' he observed, 'if it could have been continued long enough and in sufficient weight, might in the end have forced the enemy to capitulate, his counter-measures would have prevented us from maintaining such a policy to the decisive point. We would have been forced to precision attack to maintain the air situation needed to continue the offensive at all.' But he did not mean precision bombing against cities. While Germany may have been alarmed by the attacks on Hamburg and Berlin and other cities, there was no evidence, Portal maintained, to show that she was near to collapse. 'She weathered successfully the storm of the subsequent Berlin attacks.' Portal was entirely justified in reminding Harris that although ball-bearings had been selected as primary objectives as far back as mid-1943, and two raids had been carried out soon afterwards, no more attacks had been made on them until 1944 and even then no more than 3,000 tons of bombs had been used. 'I should have thought', he wrote to Harris, 'that at least you would have tried harder to destroy the Schweinfurt.' Albert Speer's subsequent comments are startlingly relevant. He recalled that the raids of August and October 1943 had reduced ball-bearing production by respectively 38 and 67 per cent. In February 1944 further raids on Schweinfurt, Erkner, Steyr and Canstatt cut production by 71 per cent. But Allied policy saved German production. 'At the beginning of April 1944,' Speer noted, 'the attacks on the ball-bearing industry ceased abruptly. Thus, the Allies threw away success when it was already in their hands. Had they continued the attacks of March and April with the same energy, we would quickly have been at our last gasp.' Speer remembered too in spite of himself the fascination of the air raids on Berlin – an unforgettable sight:

> I had constantly to remind myself of the cruel reality in order not to be completely entranced by the scene: the illumination of the parachute flares, which the Berliners called Christmas trees, followed by flashes of explosions which were caught by the clouds of smoke, the innumerable probing searchlights, the excitement when a plane was caught and tried to escape the cone of light, the brief flaming torch when it was hit. No doubt about it, this apocalypse provided a magnificent spectacle.

Not all those in Berlin had the grandstand view which Speer enjoyed from a flak tower near his office. Yet Berliners have always been renowned for their cynical and stalwart acceptance of harsh realities. As late as February 1945 their spirit was as undaunted as ever. An official in the Foreign Ministry, Hans-Georg von Studnitz, recalled that even with the Russians across the Oder, the population remained calm. Their grim humour evoked such comments that until you could reach the Eastern front by the *U-bahn*, the underground railway, the situation could not be thought of as really critical. Then again, it would be just as well to go on believing in final victory in order to save oneself from getting strung up. Moreover, the barricades would certainly save Berlin, for when the Russians saw them, they would die of laughter. They needed their spirits and resilience, their determination and humour. von Studnitz remembered a raid in early February:

> The attack began at 10.45 am and ended at 12.30. The Adlon shelter is a foot deep in water that has leaked through from the melting snow above. Many people had to wade about underground for two hours in icy water. Under the heavy explosions the massive shelter swayed and shivered like the cellar of an ordinary house.

Finally all the lights went out, and we felt as though we had been buried alive ... Gigantic clouds of smoke hung over the whole city.

Ursula von Kardorff, a journalist in Berlin, saw it all too. She remembered that on Hitler's birthday the ruins of the city had been decorated with gay little paper flags. Streamers invited the Führer to command. They would follow. Walls might be breaking but not their hearts. After the same heaviest of all raids that von Studnitz described, Ursula von Kardorff noted in her diary: 'Why does nobody go crazy? Why does nobody go out in the streets and shout "I've had enough!" Why is there not a revolution?' Meanwhile the news sheet continued – with exhortations to stick it out, to hold fast – not merely because of stories about the Russians' atrocious behaviour, but because Goebbels despite all the probabilities persisted in maintaining that victory was but a step away. 'We shall win because we must win.' Yet the Russians were only some 40 miles from the city. How long would it take them to reach it? Some said the war could only last another three days,* others put it at a fortnight. Surprisingly enough it was nearly three months away. Why, when it had taken the Russians only three weeks to advance 300 miles, did it take them three months to advance little more than 30?

It was not because of German defensive plans. There were at this time no proper plans to defend Germany west of the Oder, still less to make Berlin a fortress. That this was so was, of course, because of Hitler's refusal to recognize that such measures would be necessary. Although in his heart of hearts he may have acknowledged such a requirement, he was certainly not going to make public the imminence of the Red Army's arrival at the capital of the Third Reich. Indeed as we have seen, it was attack not defence that obsessed him. Even after the Ardennes failure, arranging for the recapture of Budapest was more in his mind than preventing the capture of Berlin.

But the truth was that if the Oder itself could not be successfully defended, the battle for Germany and for Berlin was already lost. After the war was over Jodl admitted that the German General Staff knew that it was on the Oder that the fate of Berlin would be decided. It was for this reason that those forces assembled for the city's defence were despatched east of it and, by virtue of this commitment, dissipated before the battle for the city itself was properly joined. It was not until mid-January that Keitel passed on Hitler's agreement that OKH could begin to issue the necessary orders for the military district which

*Entry in Ursula von Kardorff's diary for 8 February 1945.

included Berlin, *Wehrkreis* III, to get on with its actual preparations for defence including fortifications. Typical of Hitler's continued attempt to maintain tight personal control over *all* operations, the commander of *Wehrkreis* III was instructed to report directly to the Führer and attend his daily briefings at Hitler's headquarters. By these actions even the Supreme Commander of the Wehrmacht was making it clear that, despite the political and public propaganda disadvantages of doing so, he had admitted the existence of a threat to the capital of his Germany. Was the threat in fact an immediate one?

When we recall that the great Soviet offensive of 12 January had had as its ultimate objective the river Elbe, we might suppose that it was. Yet in fact in this respect the Soviet High Command, according to General Shtemenko,* who served in the Operations Branch of the General Staff, was labouring under comparable difficulties as those brought about by OKW's contradictory and unrealistic orders. Shtemenko has it that Konev and Zhukov in the respective and separate 1st Ukrainian and 1st Belorussian *fronts* were both aiming at Berlin :

> The offensive of Soviet troops on East Prussia, on the Vistula and in Silesia had been so decisive and precipitous that within two weeks the First Belorussian and First Ukrainian *fronts* had achieved their aims, reaching the Poznan-Breslau line. Since they had completed the first stage of the campaign, it was necessary to determine the next move immediately now that the attack on Berlin had become the order of the day and was, as you might say, our immediate goal.

> On 26 January the General Staff learned of the decision made by the commander of the First Belorussian *front* (Zhukov) to continue his offensive without halt until he captured the German capital. He proposed taking four days to move up his troops, particularly his artillery and rear services, to replenish his supplies, to get his mechanized units into order, to put the Third Shock Army and the First Polish Army into the first echelon, and on 1-2 February to renew the offensive with all his forces. His first objective was to force the Oder on the march, following up with a swift blow at Berlin, directing the chief force of his attack on the German capital from the northeast, the north and the northwest. To achieve this, the Second Guards Tank Army would strike from the northwest and the First Guards Tank Army from the northeast. The next day (27 January)

*Shtemenko made known his views on the Berlin battles in the *Voyenno-Istoricheskii Zhurnal* (the Military History Journal) of May 1965.

the General Staff received the decision of the commander of the First Ukrainian *front* (Konev) to move on his front without measurable pause, launching an offensive on 5–6 February that would reach the Elbe by 25–28 February, while his right wing, in cooperation with the First Belorussian *front*, captured Berlin.

Thus both *fronts* aimed to take Berlin without any kind of pause. But how could Marshal Konev's plan be reconciled with Stalin's orders that Berlin was to be taken by the First Belorussian *front* and that *front* only? After heated debates in General Antonev's offices the General Staff decided to approve both plans, and Supreme Headquarters agreed to this. However, the demarcation line between the two fronts was to be the one recommended by Marshal Zhukov – that is, the line that had previously been approved was to stay in effect up to the Smigiel. Beyond that the line was to be Unruhstadt-Obra River-Oder River-Ratzdorf-Friedland-Gross Köris-Michendorf. In fact, this line pushed the troops of the First Ukrainian *front* south of Berlin and gave them no opening for a direct blow from the south or southwest, compelling them to advance towards Guben and Brandenburg. The General Staff knew that this was absurd – on the one hand approving the plan of Marshal Konev for his right wing to attack Berlin and on the other establishing a demarcation line that would not permit him to carry out his plan. We had to find some way out of this situation, and we believed that either the situation itself would provide its own needed correction or that we would be able to correct this stupidity in some way in the course of the operation, particularly since we were still some distance from Berlin. But, as the evolution of events disclosed, it proved impossible to carry out the attack on Berlin in so short a time.

So wrote Shtemenko. Was then the whole question an academic one? Was it that plans for taking Berlin made in late January for execution in February were so much rubbish, for there was no possibility of their being realized? Marshal Chuikov, who commanded the 8th Guards Army, the forces directly opposite Berlin during the actual battle for it and whose troops actually occupied the city centre, seemed to think not. As late as 1964 he asserted that Berlin could have been taken in February 1945 and that with its capture the war would have ended earlier. If by this, and always assuming that the city had actually fallen and that Hitler had stuck to his determination to stay in it, he meant that the one thing which kept Germany at war at all, the Führer himself, would have obligingly removed himself from the scene, would have gone off to study a long silence, then we may assume his assertion to have some claim to be seriously considered. But it is absurd to suppose that as long as there was life and breath in the body of Adolf Hitler and that as long as he was still able to dispose the means of waging war – fire power, manoeuvrability and the communications to give effect to these two elements of combat, these two ingredients of violence – he would voluntarily have chucked in his hand and allowed himself to be taken, to have become the gaped-at show piece of the age. Equally unlikely is that there would have been any lack of generals to obey his instructions to continue with the final tragic act of Götterdämmerung. The key question remains – could the Red Army have taken Berlin earlier than they did?

With certain qualifications Professor Ziemke, the American historian, endorses Chuikov's view that they could have done so. While Chuikov maintained that what prevented the continued Russian advance was Stalin's veto on it and his order to reorganize and consolidate on the River Oder, his superior commander Zhukov remarkably enough denies having even contemplated a drive straight to Berlin – despite the General Staff's record of his having recommended and planned for this very course of action. The reason Zhukov gave was that the state of his armies after this 300-mile advance from the Vistula to the Oder – all in less than three weeks – had rendered their condition such that they could not undertake so grandiose a further operation. Moreover Zhukov claimed that the German threat to the north, that is from Pomerania, was far too great to allow him so to expose his flanks. There are two points here. Firstly the state of his troops early in February could well have led Zhukov to conclude that the second great phase of the Red Army's offensive might have to be postponed – but this is a far cry from denying that it had even been contemplated. Secondly, what of the threat from the north? Was it really so substantial, were the German forces there so balanced, well supplied and fit for a proper counter attack, that despite the Russians astonishing successes in destroying and disrupting the Wehrmacht's Eastern front, they could not have been contained on the northern flank by say Rokossovsky's Second Belorussian *front*, while Zhukov and Konev pressed on? It may be doubted. Far more probable an explanation is to be found in the working of Stalin's mind. Was he, as Hitler was in 1940, unnerved by his own success, reluctant to extend his forces still further lest some drastic counter blow by the never to be despised Guderian cut the head off the advancing bear? Or was it that, certain of being able to take

Berlin whenever he wanted it, and perhaps sanguine that its capture would end the war, he was happy enough actually to *prolong* the conflict in order to ensure that other desirable objectives – on the Baltic coast for example or in south-eastern and central-eastern Europe – should fall into the hands of his armies rather than those of his Allies? The very insignificance of the German threat in the north at this time might lead us to suppose that it was not Stalin's fear about failing to capture Berlin that held him back, but more the certainty that Berlin would be his whenever he decided that the time was right. All the Germans could muster in Pomerania and West Prussia during the first week of February which might have done damage to the Russians was the remnants of the 2nd Army reinforced by what scattered troops had escaped the mighty hammer blows dealt them since 12 January. But opportunities in war do not commonly recur. Tides ebb, floods recede, shallows follow. Once the decision not to go on during the first week of February had been taken, other influences made themselves felt. The German plans, however depleted their means of effecting them, could not be ignored altogether.

It may be supposed that no German plans could have made any difference to the outcome of the war itself : it was clearly lost, had long been lost. Nevertheless the way in which it was finally lost was still open to manipulation. The first few days of February 1945 were not exactly promising ones from the German point of view. In the east the flood-gates had finally cracked. The Russians were on, even across, the Oder. East Prussia and Upper Silesia were gone, so that Berlin, West Prussia, Pomerania, indeed all parts of Germany were at the mercy of the Red Army. All that stood between them and an advance up to where the Western Allies themselves were – still broadly on the line of the Rhine – were Wehrmacht formations already shattered by three weeks fighting for the Vistula and a makeshift Army Group commanded by the totally unqualified Himmler. 'If the Russians maintained their rate of advance,' wrote Professor Ziemke in summing up the situation, 'and there seemed to be no reason why they could not, they would be on the Rhine in another three weeks.'

In such predicaments the Supreme Commander of the Wehrmacht, Adolf Hitler, was at his most and least effective. At his best he refused to despair or give up. What is more he refused to allow others to do so. Such was the extraordinary grip he still maintained on his subordinates and on the Wehrmacht as a whole, such was the habit of accepting Hitler's absolute and eccentric control of the whole nation's military resources that this refusal to face the facts and ability to draw comfort

Russian troops in East Prussia

German troops captured in Roer battles

British troops—Rhine battles

from resolution alone somehow persuaded others that all was not lost. At his worst he then made plans and gave orders so unrelated to the military capability of either side that any advantage gained from unshakable willpower was at once dissipated by ensuring failure in the subsequent operations. Nor was he prepared to keep his eye on the principal issue – the threat to Berlin. He still pursued chimerical and irrelevant sideshows elsewhere.

It is important to remember too the method of command which Hitler exercised. In the first place his insistence on controlling events in one sense prevailed to the very end even though paradoxically enough it allowed control of these events to pass to the other side. Secondly, by laying down that withdrawals to new positions would only be authorized by himself, he made sure that the picture presented to him of the front was of the very circumstances which he himself had defined as being necessary to justify withdrawal. In his analysis of Hitler as a military leader, Professor Percy Ernst Schramm, who kept the official war diary of OKW from the beginning of 1943 until 1945, gives us a number of examples of how Hitler's conduct of war had its effect on the way in which the Commanders-in-Chief who served him adjusted their methods in order as far as possible to retain some freedom of action.

Field-Marshal von Rundstedt, who had been dismissed and recalled again more often than most of the senior German commanders and who was at this time Commander-in-Chief, West, had learned this trick of singularity. He would somehow turn the commonplace into the remarkable, make his proposals palatable, frame his reports in such a way that on one hand he seemed to be conforming to Hitler's general strategy in just the way the Führer intended, but on the other gave himself the tactical freedom indispensable to the successful conduct of any warlike operations. He was in the middle of coping with the Western Allies battle for the Rhineland and on 9 February 1945 he submitted a request to OKW for authority to make minor withdrawals in order to straighten and strengthen the front in such terms – reassuring the Führer that such moves would only be contemplated in order to maintain the front's cohesion and that any broader strategic implications would instantly be made known to him – that on the following day his request was granted. Even then he was forbidden to evacuate any city or fortification. These, no matter how attacked or stormed, would never be abandoned 'except by order of the Führer'.

By these methods Hitler guaranteed for himself the spirit of obedience and the letter of evasion. Yet at the beginning of February 1945 we are faced with the extraordinary situation that, while Berlin is still clearly the prime military objective simply because it contained the Führer, Stalin seems to have turned away from it, the Western Allies have no firm plans to take it, and Hitler himself is still more concerned with counter-attacking elsewhere than ensuring its proper defence. It was not clear even now who would get there first. No doubt the coming battles of February and March would make it so.

6

THE EASTERN FRONT

For the German nation, 'the war' meant the war in the East. The bombing, the U-boat campaign, the glamour of the Afrika Korps, these were incidentals when over two million fathers, husbands and brothers were engaged day and night in a struggle with the Untermensch.

ALAN CLARK

On 12 January 1945 the greatest offensive launched by any army at any time in the Second World War began. The numbers involved spoke for themselves. In Zhukov's 1st Belorussian *front* and Konev's 1st Ukrainian *front* alone there were roughtly 160 divisions, over 30,000 guns, nearly 6,500 tanks and self-propelled guns, the best part of 5,000 aircraft and more than two million men. It had all been repeatedly predicted by Guderian's Intelligence Officer, General Gehlen – predictions as repeatedly brushed aside by Hitler. When we remember that also taking part were two other Russian *fronts*, 2nd Belorussian to the north of Zhukov and 4th Ukrainian to the south of Konev, to say nothing of the 1st Polish Army, and that opposing this giant steam-roller were some 60 German divisions with a dozen in reserve, we may appreciate Guderian's answer to Hitler on 9 January, three days before the offensive started. Having categorically refused Guderian's request either to reinforce the Eastern front from the West or to allow adjustments to present German deployment, Hitler tried to console Guderian with a small piece of soft soap: 'The Eastern front has never before possessed such a strong reserve as now. That is your doing. I thank you for it.' Guderian's reply was not designed to console and it did not. 'The Eastern front is like a house of cards. If the front is broken through at one point all the rest will collapse, for twelve and a half divisions are far too small a reserve for so extended a front.'

Sure enough when the time came the Eastern front revealed the fragility emphasized by Guderian and went down with all the speed

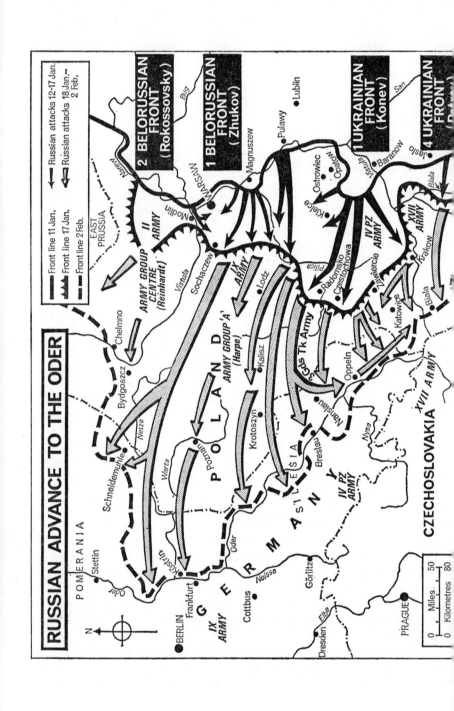

RUSSIAN ADVANCE TO THE ODER

Front line 11 Jan.
Front line 17 Jan.
Front line 2 Feb.
Russian attacks 12-17 Jan.
Russian attacks 18 Jan.-2 Feb.

2 BELORUSSIAN FRONT (Rokossovsky)

1 BELORUSSIAN FRONT (Zhukov)

1 UKRAINIAN FRONT (Konev)

4 UKRAINIAN FRONT (Petrov)

EAST PRUSSIA

ARMY GROUP CENTRE (Reinhardt)

II ARMY

Lublin

Pulawy

Magnuszew

Ostrowiec

Opatow

Lublin

Baranow

Kielce

Kraków

Biala

Vistula

San

Dunajec

XVII ARMY

IV PZ ARMY

Radomsko

Częstochowa

Zawiercie

Katowice

Oppeln

Biala

3Gds Tk Army

IV PZ ARMY

CZECHOSLOVAKIA

XVII ARMY

Nysa

Neisse

Nysa

Breslau

Namslau

Krotoszyn

Kalisz

Lodz

Pilica

Radomsko

Sochaczew

Modlin

WARSAW

Narew

Bug

Vistula

ARMY GROUP 'A' (Harpe)

IX ARMY

Chelmno

Bydgoszcz

Netze

Warta

POLAND

Poznan

Oder

S I L E S I A

G E R M A N Y

Schneidemühle

Küstrin

Frankfurt

BERLIN

IX ARMY

Stettin

Oder

POMERANIA

Cottbus

Görlitz

Elbe

Dresden

PRAGUE

N

0   50 Miles
0   80 Kilometres

and thoroughness of a house of cards. Very broadly what happened in the Vistula-Oder battle was this. Konev's 1st Ukrainian *front* led the way in breaking out of their Baranov bridgehead while Zhukov's 1st Belorussian *front* broke out of their Pulavy and Magnuszev bridgeheads across the Vistula. Together in a series of huge and fast encircling movements they simply overwhelmed General Harpe's Army Group A.

Guderian's description of the Eastern front as a house of cards was apt not only in depicting its general structural weakness, but more particularly in the point he made that if you removed one part of it the whole thing would disintegrate since there was no central, pliable and resilient core which could, as it were, react without losing purpose, recoil without being stampeded. This point is well illustrated by Konev's assault from the Baranov bridgehead. The defending German formations, 48 and 24 Panzer Corps with perhaps six of seven under-strength divisions and a mere handful of guns, were incapable of putting together the only sort of defence which has a chance of fighting successfully, that is to say a series of mutually supporting positions in depth which can by their joint strength deliver more and more powerful blows on the advancing enemy troops to take the steam out of them and eventually halt the attack altogether. The most the German defenders could muster was a string of uncoordinated, independent strongpoints all of which were liable to defeat in detail. When we consider that against this defence Konev was able to mount five infantry armies and two tank armies, with over 400 guns deployed to every mile of front and over 1000 tanks to play with, it is hardly surprising that these armies made holes everywhere in the German defences and then drove straight through them. The same story was told all along the Eastern front.

In the north Rokossovsky pushed back and cut off the remnants of General Reinhardt's Army Group Centre. Within a few weeks Zhukov and Konev were on the Oder and Rokossovsky almost on the Baltic having isolated East Prussia. Guderian had long been trying to adjust matters in order to avoid just these circumstances. Gehlen had convinced him that the coming Soviet offensive would be in the sort of strength to bring about the collapse of Army Group Centre's position. The choice was a very simple one. Either the Germans would conduct an orderly withdrawal from positions held and so aim to preserve the hinterland of East Prussia, or East Prussia would have to be abandoned and thus give the troops some badly needed respite. It escaped neither Guderian nor Gehlen that the loss of East Prussia would not mean final defeat whereas a continued successful Soviet offensive would. So Guderian from his headquarters at Zossen struggled in vain to make bricks without straw, and at the same time appealed to the Führer – who until 15 January was still at *Adlershorst*, the Führer's headquarters in Hesse from where he had directed and misdirected the Ardennes offensive – for reinforcements. As early as 13 January Guderian was aware of the gigantic strength of the Russian forces opposing him. In the Baranov-Kielce thrust by Konev, he later recorded, a total of 32 rifle divisions and eight tank corps were employed – 'the greatest concentration of force in the narrowest area that had been seen since the beginning of the war'. By 15 January the general pattern of the Russian offensive had become clear to Guderian. The main enemy thrusts, south to north, were from Jaslow to Cracow, from Baranov to Kielce and beyond to join up with the next northernmost thrust from Pulavy, from Magnuszev to Warsaw, and from the Bug-Vistula triangle north-west to the Baltic. 'Needless to say,' wrote Guderian

> from the beginning of the great Russian offensive I had kept Hitler fully and frankly informed by telephone of the grave developments taking place, and had urgently requested that he return at once to Berlin and thus at least demonstrate that our main defensive effort was now in the East. His replies during the first few days consisted merely of a constant repetition of the instructions he had given me on 9 January: 'The Eastern front must make do with what it's got.'

On 15 January, however, Hitler began to interfere and sent orders that *Gross-Deutschland* Panzer Corps, consisting of a Panzergrenadier Division and a Panzer Parachute division and Corps troops, should be transferred from East Prussia to try and stop the Russian drive in the Kielce area. This in Guderian's view would simply be to rob Peter without being able to pay Paul. The ensuing argument between them resulted in the absurdity of this powerful Panzer Corps wasting its time in railway sidings having no influence on either battle while arguments about its destination proceeded. It was Grouchy at Waterloo all over again. On this same day Hitler decided to quit *Adlershorst* and reached Berlin the following day, 16 January, never to leave again. His broad decision was that the Western Front must go over to the defensive in order to allow strengthening of the East. This principle of course was most acceptable to Guderian, but when he heard that Hitler wished to send Dietrich's 6th Panzer Army not to the critical central area, but to

Hungary, he exploded with anger – to no effect. Hitler seemed more interested in relieving Budapest than in safeguarding his own country and capital. At this time some Commanders were replaced by others, as if to indicate that the fault lay not in Hitler's strategy but in those who were failing to carry it out properly. Schörner replaced Harpe in command of Army Group A, within which Busse took over 9th Army from von Lüttwitz. But no changes in command, no identification of supposed scapegoats, could alter the facts that Army Group North in Courland was in danger of being cut off. Indeed on 17 January Gehlen again warned that Marshal Bagramyan was about to start an attack designed to destroy Army Group North and advance deep into the Reich. A similar report by Gehlen before Christmas had been torn up by Hitler. He had condemned the report as the biggest bluff since Genghis Khan. 'What idiot has dug up this rubbish?' Now he could not dismiss it so easily for it had become plain that unless more defensive troops were produced for the Central area, not Hitler, nor Guderian, nor anyone else could stop the Russians from closing in on the homeland of Germany.

On 20 January they did so, and for the first time the Red Army was on German soil.* They continued to eat it up. By 23 January, as Zhukov later recorded in pointing out that his *front* had improved on the timetable laid down by the Stavka, 'the *front's* right wing had already seized Bydgoszez and had developed the offensive toward Schneidemühl and Deutsch-Krone. On 25 January the centre of the *front* surrounded powerful forces at Poznan, and the left wing, closely coordinated with the 1st Ukrainian *front*, advanced to the region of Jarocin.' At this point in a conversation with Stalin on 25 January Zhukov made it plain that he intended to advance to the Oder, seize a bridgehead at Küstrin, then with his right wing turn north and northwest to deal with German forces in East Pomerania. Stalin, however, vetoed the last proposal in that Rokossovsky's 2nd Belorussian *front* would not have finished mopping up East Prussia. Therefore Zhukov would have to wait for his advance beyond the Oder until Rokossovsky had regrouped on the Vistula. In this lack of close coordination between the two Russian *fronts* lay a possibility for a counter-stroke by the Germans.

By 25 January Guderian had proposed and got Hitler to agree to a new command arrangement. The former Army Group A had been redesigned Army Group Centre, and what had been Army Group

---

*Where it has remained ever since. It would be a bold man who could forecast when if ever it will leave.

Centre became Army Group North. To defend the area between them, Guderian formed a new Army Group Vistula and proposed to give it to Field-Marshal von Weichs. It seems clear that Guderian really intended himself to direct the operations of Army Group Vistula which would counter attack the Russian troops preparing to advance along the Vistula's west bank. But to his consternation and horror, Hitler appointed – Himmler! As if sending the bulk of his panzer reinforcements from the West to Hungary were not enough to ensure catastrophe on the Vistula, Hitler completed the process by appointing the former sergeant-major to command of an Army Group. 'This preposterous suggestion appalled me,' wrote Guderian, 'and I used such argumentative powers as I possessed in an attempt to stop such idiocy being perpetrated on the unfortunate Eastern Front. It was all in vain.' Guderian did not even succeed, at least not at first, in arranging for some proper military advice to be made available to the pitiless, arrogant, ignorant and mystical Reichsführer. Himmler chose his own SS subordinates in accordance with Hitler's wish that this should be an SS Army, that is to say, one that could be trusted to make good the fumbling failures and endless treasons of the professional soldiers.

On that same day, 25 January, Guderian tried to persuade the egregiously blundering Ribbentrop of the need to approach Hitler and make him face the fact of impending collapse and disaster. Ribbentrop's initial reaction was to ask whether the General Staff was losing its nerve. Even the resolute Guderian could not help recording in his memoirs that it would have required nerves of cast-iron to conduct such conversations and at the same time think clearly and keep cool. What Guderian was after – utterly fruitless though it was in the sense of inducing either Hitler to try it or the Allies to accede to it – was an armistice in the West so that he would be able to transfer such a weight of the Wehrmacht to the East, that the Russian steam-roller could be stopped. When Ribbentrop refused, Guderian asked him how he would feel if in three or four weeks time the Russians were at the gates of Berlin, and on Ribbentrop's horrified question as to whether he thought that likely, rubbed home the point by saying that the nation's leadership had made it certain. His estimate was only two months out. That night Hitler, who by then had heard from Ribbentrop what had happened, raged at Guderian for being guilty of high treason.

So it went on from day to day – Guderian trying to make what he could out of an almost hopeless military situation, Hitler insisting on sending what reinforcements were arriving from the West to irrelevant areas in the south, Guderian trying to draw in horns while they might yet be drawn in and used for the critical battles opposite Berlin which were yet to come, Hitler insisting on holding on everywhere, and meanwhile the Red Army growing ever bolder, advancing and continuing to advance. By the end of January and beginning of February the Russians were still attacking and being successful everywhere – between the Danube and Lake Balaton, across the Oder* at Küstrin, at the Oder-Warthe bend, in Courland. Königsberg was cut off, Stettin threatened. Zhukov's only concern was that resistance on his right was hardening and therefore Rokossovsky on the right was ordered to resume the offensive. Meanwhile at a conference on 27 January the best thing that Hitler could think of was :

> I have ordered that a report be played into their [the British] hands to the effect that the Russians are organizing 200,000 of our men, led by German officers and completely infected with Communism, who will then be marched into Germany ... That will make them feel as if someone has stuck a needle into them.

Propaganda of this sort had done much in the past. It could do nothing now. Far more to the point were Guderian's attempts to use 6th Panzer Army and all other available reinforcements in order to attack the exposed Russian spearheads in Pomerania east of the Oder and in the Glogau-Kottbus area on the Oder southeast of Küstrin and Frankfurt. But no, they were to be employed in Hungary – not however before March. 'How', asked Guderian, 'was Berlin to manage until then?' When the Russians had actually reached the Küstrin-Frankfurt area during the first week of February, Guderian tried again. 6th Panzer Army was still uncommitted together with the best part of two panzer divisions at Krampnitz. But, insisted Guderian, when he tried to persuade Hitler to counter-attack the Russian flanks of their central thrust towards Berlin, Courland would have to be evacuated. This, together with Guderian's explanation that he saw no other way of assembling sufficient reserves to defend Berlin itself and that he was thinking only of Germany's interests, produced an even more spectacular and alarming outburst on Hitler's part : 'How dare you speak to me like that? Don't you think I'm fighting for Germany? My whole life has been one

---

*One report by Gehlen's staff about the Russians crossing the Oder at Lucken was, it seems, concealed from Hitler for some weeks. He was understandably incensed and in one of the last War Directives promised 'draconian punishment' for any future attempts at concealment, demanding also that every report made to him by no matter whom should contain 'nothing but the unvarnished truth'. The absurdities had come full circle. Previously he had furiously rejected the truth. Now he complained that no one told it to him.

long struggle for Germany.' General Thomale, Guderian's principal
Staff Officer, even had to grip his chief's jacket and pull him back out of
range of the Führer's fists.

Yet in spite of all this Guderian had his way with plans to launch an
attack from the Arnswalde area on the Russian spearheads north of the
Warthe in order to keep Pomerania and to remain in touch with West
Prussia. This attack was planned for mid-February by which time the
Russians had slowed down and were consolidating on the general line
Breslau-Küstrin-Danzig. It would be conducted by Army Group
Vistula still under Himmler, and Guderian when he attended Hitler's
conference on 13 February was anxious first that Wenck, his principal
assistant, should be in charge of actual operations – the only hope of
Guderian's own tactical ideas prevailing and thus of any likely success
– and secondly that the attack should be launched on 15 February
before the Russians had time further to reinforce the front. Not surprisingly he was opposed on both these points by the Führer, who
supported Himmler's view that since not all the petrol and ammunition
had been issued to the troops, the attack should be postponed. When
Guderian pointed out that they could not wait until every shell and can
of fuel had been delivered, Hitler forbade Guderian to accuse him of
wanting to wait. When Guderian stated that Wenck must be attached
to Himmler's headquarters, otherwise the attack could not possibly succeed, since neither Himmler nor his staff had the necessary experience,
Hitler replied that he did not permit Guderian so to belittle Himmler.
On and on for two hours the discussion went, Hitler striding up and
down, trembling all over when he halted in front of Guderian to
scream insults and accusations in his face, eyes popping and veins
standing out in his head. It was all most disagreeable. Yet Guderian
stuck to his guns, and in the end Hitler climbed down and told
Himmler that Wenck would arrive at his headquarters that evening
and take charge of operations. The extraordinary aftermath was that
Hitler, quite calm again by now, gave Guderian a charming smile as
he announced that the General Staff had just won a battle. It was,
Guderian commented, the last battle he won and it was in any case
much too late.

The battle itself which began on 16 February was to start with a
moderate success. 3rd Panzer Army with six panzer divisions, but without air support, advanced against fairly light Russian infantry forces
supported by some anti-tank guns, and took several thousand prisoners.
But on the second evening Wenck had a motor accident. Being required
to attend Hitler's evening conferences, he had to drive from Stettin,

Army Group Headquarters, to Berlin, which were 100 miles apart. On his way back to his headquarters on 17 February he took the wheel himself because the driver was exhausted, fell asleep, crashed into a bridge on the autobahn and was seriously injured. He was replaced by General Hans Krebs, a 'smooth surviving type', one of Hitler's men. So Guderian lost control of Army Group Vistula, and Krebs lost control of the operation which quickly bogged down. Alan Clark described it as the last German offensive of the war : 'it lasted four days – the shortest as well as the least successful offensive undertaken by the German Army.' At this point in the war even a multiplicity of equipment, superb planning and brilliant united leadership could hardly have prevailed against the Red Army. It was therefore unlikely that the very reverse of these conditions would do so.

With the last of the German offensives in the east, or anywhere else for that matter, shown to be a failure, what was to be done? The Red Army was halted, it was tired and it might be that before long a thaw would set in to slow down their further advance. But what then? What sort of military operations could be conducted by the Wehrmacht which had any relevance to the future? Hitler had always maintained that there would be no surrender, no question of besmirching the nation's honour a second time. If then he were obliged to abandon his first alternative – *Weltmacht,* world power – it looked uncomfortably as if the second, *Niedergang,* ruin, was all that was left. Very well ! But if Germany were to be conquered, then Germany would make sure that there was no one left to triumph over her. It was in a recurrence of this sort of mood that Hitler would make such monstrous statements as 'if the German people loses the war, it will have proved itself not worthy of me' and that 'if the war is lost, the nation must perish'. Nihilism as an end in itself took possession of him as did the idea that the fault lay not with himself, principal perpetrator of it all, but with the German people.

But perhaps the most astonishing feature of the whole lurid picture at this time, when it was clear that the war was lost, was Hitler's ability to sustain some shred of hope in others. As late as 24 February 1945 in addressing the Gauleiter – it was the twenty-fifth anniversary of the first massed Nazi meeting – he was somehow able to inspire a sort of confidence in them that all would yet be well. Even more than two months later and within a few days of his own death, with the Red Army investing Berlin, the Chancellory itself under bombardment by Russian guns, and the end of the whole game in sight, we find Field-Marshal Ritter von Greim telephoning from the bunker to General

Koller giving prophecies and promises of victory. He had been inspired by the presence and confidence of the Führer and therefore everything would yet go well. But make no mistake, if it did not go well, more blood would be spilled. Quite apart from that inflicted on other nations – there were seven million Russians killed alone – Hitler had not done badly by his own. After all, he had inflicted on them the best part of ten million casualties. Perhaps therefore no matter what else happened, some sort of *Lebensraum* would be achieved – not by gaining possession of territory in the east, but simply by a general reduction of the number of Germans requiring space in which to live.

In spite of the huge advances of the Russian Armies since the beginning of their Vistula-Oder offensive, some 300 miles in less than three weeks, they had halted, and were reorganizing, consolidating, closing up on the flanks and preparing for the next move. Except for East Prussia, invasion of the Third Reich itself had only just started. On the other side of Germany, the Western Allies were similarly only just beginning to get their feet on to German soil, and were more than 200 miles from the German capital. Yet the Russians were a mere 40 miles from Berlin. Would the battle for Berlin precede the battle for Germany, or would its fall render the battle for Germany unnecessary? Indeed what were the Western Allies' aims at this point in the war – simply to go on hammering and destroying the German armies until they no longer resisted, crush them between themselves and the Red Army, make a dash for Berlin and beat the Red Army there or what? There were those who were raising again the question of the National Redoubt, the so called last-stand area of National Socialism in the Bavarian mountains. Now that the nutcracker was at last beginning to close, was it quite clear where or even what the nut would be? And how was Eisenhower proposing to crack it?

7

THE WESTERN FRONT

But what he has up front are not divisions. They're just rubbish. All the same, he has to make something out of that rubbish.*

HITLER, Führer Conference, March 1945

War in Europe is very often a matter of crossing rivers and there is usually one more to cross. In pursuit of his declared intentions General Eisenhower had first to close up to the Rhine, then cross it, and then advance from it. Clearly the way in which he wished to do the last of these would influence his methods of tackling the other two. All three were in accordance with his long since decided strategy. Yet his proposals were the cause of violent disagreement by one of his principal American subordinates, Bradley. At this time Eisenhower still intended that his main effort beyond the Rhine should be made in the north, that is on Montgomery's front because it was from the Lower Rhine north of the Ruhr that his forces would most quickly be able to thrust into the North German Plain which offered the great advantages of good going for fast moving armoured forces and of most rapidly removing from the Germans the sinews of war produced by the Ruhr industries. At the same time, as we have seen, a secondary advance directed via Frankfurt on Kassel was to be made so that the Ruhr could be completely encircled. Thereafter Eisenhower saw it as his purpose to link up with the Russians. There was also the question of what Devers, the third of Eisenhower's Army Group commanders, would be doing in the south, and this would largely depend on what forces were available. Bradley's objections were based not on military reasoning but on national susceptibilities. His whole concept of strategy was coloured by his insistence that since the Americans were providing the bulk of the troops and resources, everything connected with strategy – concentra-

*Hitler was referring to the military position of 19th Army in the Upper Rhine area.

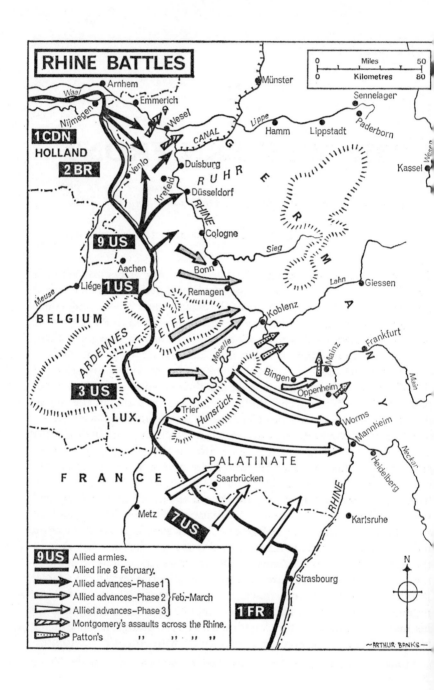

RHINE BATTLES

Münster
Sennelager
Arnhem
Waal
Emmerich
Wesel
Lippe
Hamm
Lippstadt
Paderborn
Nijmegen
CANAL
1 CDN
HOLLAND
Duisburg
Kassel
2 BR
Venlo
RUHR
Krefeld
Düsseldorf
RHINE
Cologne
9 US
Aachen
Siegburg
Bonn
Liége
1 US
Remagen
Koblenz
Giessen
BELGIUM
EIFEL
Lahn
Frankfurt
ARDENNES
Moselle
Mainz
Main
3 US
Bingen
Oppenheim
LUX.
Trier
Hunsrück
Worms
Mannheim
PALATINATE
Heidelberg
Neckar
F R A N C E
Saarbrücken
Metz
7 US
Karlsruhe

N

9 US	Allied armies.
▬▬	Allied line 8 February.
➤	Allied advances—Phase 1
➤	Allied advances—Phase 2 }Feb.–March
➤	Allied advances—Phase 3
▨➤	Montgomery's assaults across the Rhine.
▱➤	Patton's " " " "

Strasbourg

1 FR

~ARTHUR BANKS~

Miles
0 50
Kilometres
0 80

tion of troops for the final blow, their command, the plan, its execution and resultant triumphs – all should be American too. He could not see that concentration in the centre instead of the north was not merely subject to the same criticism as its alternative. It was subject to even more objection in that the central sector was much easier to defend by virtue of the terrain alone. In other words, to go head on for the strongest part of the German defences was a proposition with little to recommend it to anyone other than to Bradley himself, who was anxious to keep the Germans on the run and equally anxious to give his troops the opportunity of completely cancelling out and avenging the reverses they had undergone during the winter battles of the Ardennes. Fortunately for the Allies, Bradley's arguments did not prevail with Eisenhower who stuck to his decision to leave a substantial part of Bradley's Army Group, that is to say the 9th US Army, with Montgomery in the north.

For his advance from the Rhine into Germany Eisenhower intended to use some 35 divisions in Montgomery's main northern advance, and allotted a total of 25 for Bradley in the central area. All in all he could count on 85 divisions for this advance, so that a further 25 would be in hand for holding firm in the area between these two main offensives. All of this was contingent upon clearing the Germans completely from any areas west of the Rhine, for any footholds they might still have there would demand such numbers to contain them that there would be insufficient strength to get on with the business of crossing and advancing from the Rhine. There continued to be disagreements between the two Western Allies as to the wisdom, indeed the logistic practicability of simultaneously carrying out these two thrusts. The main British concern was that the Russians might reach the Western Baltic and North Sea ports while they were still fiddling about in the Rhineland. Therefore, the British argued, one main attack only – and that as soon as possible, by themselves, in the north with all the strength musterable – was the correct strategy. In spite of this disagreement, Eisenhower's plans, which amounted to a continuation of what had all along been his plans, advance on a broad front, were endorsed by the Combined Chiefs of Staff.

For clearing up to the Rhine itself Eisenhower's operations were to be divided into three parts: first Montgomery would capture all ground up to the west bank from Nijmegen to Düsseldorf, next Bradley would secure the area further south from Düsseldorf to Koblenz, finally the Moselle-Saar-Rhine area would be cleared by converging attacks from Patton's 3rd Army (still under Bradley's Army Group) and

Patch's 7th Army (in Devers' 6th Army Group). Bradley would also seize crossings at Mainz-Karlsruhe. We may do well to follow the fortunes of these three enterprises in relation to Hitler's reiterated determination not to give up the West Wall, that is to continue to defend Germany west of the Rhine. This was not only because of Hitler's customary insistence not to give up an inch of German soil and so on, but also because leaving aside the absolute indispensability of the Ruhr itself in producing the materials to wage war, it was in the barges of the Rhine that much of this material was transported to other areas which actually turned out the weapons.

Montgomery laid down his Army Group's task thus : 'To destroy all enemy in the area west of the Rhine from the present forward positions south of Nijmegen as far south as the general line Jülich-Düsseldorf, as a preliminary to crossing the Rhine and engaging the enemy in mobile war to the north of the Ruhr.' For these operations Montgomery had three armies – 1st Canadian, 2nd British and 9th US. Their respective jobs and resources were these. 1st Canadian Army with some 11 divisions and nine independent brigades would clear up to Xanten (Operation *Veritable*), 9th US Army with some ten divisions up to Düsseldorf (Operation *Grenade*) and 2nd British Army with rather more than four divisions would hold firm in the centre. The Allies expected to find that opposing them would be about a dozen enemy divisions and that Commander-in-Chief West, the long suffering von Rundstedt, would probably have call on the same number again from his reserves. The whole thing would begin on 8 February.

It could hardly be said that the country over which these battles were to be fought was conducive either to comfort or to mobile operations. In the first place Horrocks' 30 Corps which led the 1st Canadian Army, had to attack between two rivers, the Meuse and the Rhine, ground susceptible to flooding if the dykes were cut; secondly the Reichswald with its narrow rides had to be traversed; thirdly the Germans had had plenty of time to develop their defences and correctly anticipate the direction of the main attack, fourthly, Goch and Cleve, both natural battlements at the easterly exits of the Reichswald, had been heavily fortified; fifthly as the attack started it thawed and rained. It was hardly surprising therefore that it took Horrocks six days to clear the Reichswald.

Sir Martin Lindsay who commanded 1st Battalion, The Gordon Highlanders, had good reason to remember the Reichswald battles. He had given his orders – the battalion's task was to seize part of the Mook-Gennep road – and had noticed how quiet the Jocks were.

Remagen bridge in use by US troops

Remagen bridge after use

US airborne troops in Rhine crossing

French Army in Strasbourg

There was a good deal of unpleasant shelling before the battalion even reached the start-line, then shortly after 9 am on 9 February the battalion began its attack. At first all went fairly well and the companies advanced with artillery and tank support to their various positions en route to the final objective. But soon the battalion got bogged down by enemy mines and machine-gun fire, and then Lindsay himself moving forward with one of his companies ran into a nasty shock. How well he describes the utter fog and confusion of a battle:

Just as we got there we were ambushed. There was a burst of Schmeisser in front, and the sharp explosions of one or two German grenades. Immediately five or six Germans came to life in trenches on either side of the path. They must have been asleep, for one-third of us had already passed them. There was an instantaneous crash of automatic fire from the column and every one of them fell, riddled with bullets. It was all over in about two seconds, and our only casualty was Macpherson, slightly wounded in the leg. Actually it was a most efficient performance on our part, but all I thought at the time was: 'God, how bloody! Ambushed before we've even started, this is going to be the bloodiest show that's ever been.' . . .

Every hundred yards took us about fifteen minutes, and the confusion was indescribable. I found myself scrambling along with Porter, at the head of his platoon, he in front with an automatic very much at the ready, and me close up, keeping direction with a compass. I knew that Sergeant Matthews' platoon was just behind us; but as to where Danny and Macpherson and the rest of the company was, I hadn't a clue. All we could do was to push on slowly, climbing over tree trunks and branches or crawling under them. 'What an awful balls up of this I've made,' I thought to myself, having lost all control. 'It's going to be a ghastly failure.' . . .

I leaned against a tree and listened to Danny running the show. The same light mortar kept slamming down close to us on our left. Everybody was a bit frightened, except perhaps Danny. I heard him moving from platoon to platoon, full of confidence, putting them in position and giving orders. Then the leading platoon moved forward. 'Get on, you bastards, what the hell are you doing hanging back on the right?' I heard his loud voice shout. . . .

Danny, Porter and I were in the middle of a minefield, but fortunately those behind us were still in the old German diggings so I told them to go back. . . .

I thought there was altogether too much bustle. 'For God's sake

...' I shouted, and there was another loud bang and one of them fell down, badly injured. It now took a long time to get out the two wounded men, with every footstep being prodded first. Danny had ceased to be talkative, and I learned that he had received a lot of wood splinters in the back of the head, as Porter had in the face. When the stretcher party had left, the Canadian pioneer sergeant prodded his way up to me and led me safely out of the minefield by my planting my feet precisely in his footsteps.

By this time Macpherson, who had carried on in spite of his leg wound, had been evacuated, so D had lost all its four officers in the course of the day. I formed up the company and marched them back. I was dead tired, and felt none of the elation to which I was entitled when I reported to the Brigade that the road was now clear. . . .

Although an infantryman, Lindsay's estimate of who ranked first, second and third in danger stakes will hardly be challenged by anyone who has heard those mortal engines counterfeiting Jove's dread clamours :

Mortaring is not like shelling, you don't hear the distant whistle of the shells coming slowly from afar. There is a sudden swish and a crack as the first bomb arrives, and you have hardly any time before the others land. We would wait a few minutes half-way down the cellar steps and then I would say : 'Come on, chaps, now we'll go.' And then, when half-way over to the carrier, we would hear the swishes and the cracks, and some would drop flat while the others dodged back into the house. But it was not fun at all. In the autumn I had thought it was, but I no longer did so.

But it was far, far worse for the sappers. I took off my hat to them. It was all the same for the assault RE – either building bridges or clearing roads of mines in places where the enemy could not fail to know that we needed bridges or roads, and therefore always under fire. It was different for us, who had a job to do and then were able to dig in.

I would have put the unpleasantness, by which I mean the danger, of soldiering in this campaign as : firstly, field companies, RE; secondly, infantry; and thirdly, either airborne formations (who had long rests at home between operations, or tank crews (who were not called upon to fight so often as infantry). And the rest (with the German 1944–45 shortage of ammunition) nowhere at all in comparison.

It should be remembered that during the Reichswald battle the Germans, by virtue of having destroyed the discharge apparatus of the Roer dams, had flooded the Roer, eliminated the danger of a simultaneous or supporting attack by the American 9th Army further to the south, and so enabled themselves to concentrate further against Horrocks' Corps. But of course this very commitment of reserves made the 9th Army's attack easier when it came. Simpson's job was to clear the enemy from the Roer to the Rhine between Xanten and Düsseldorf. Beginning his attack on 23 February, he reached the Rhine south of Düsseldorf by 3 March, and had the previous day linked up with the 1st Canadian Army near Venlo.

This meant that between the two Allied Armies, a substantial German force, no fewer than 15 divisions, was trapped – unless they crossed the Rhine. But Hitler was so intent upon preserving the Rhine as a means of communication for his coal and steel that he categorically refused to consider this prudent course. His orders were couched in customarily extreme language. Not a single man, nor a single panzer or mortar or anything was to be moved east of the river without his personal and express permission. At all costs a bridgehead in the Wesel-Krefeld area was to be maintained. At the same time when the moment came to move east not a single bridge was to be allowed to fall into enemy hands. If any did the local commander would answer for it with his life.

The 4th Royal Tank Regiment was one of the armoured units supporting the infantry in their drive through the Hochwald to Xanten, and during the first ten days of March helped to clear all enemy from west of the Rhine. Right up until the last moment the enemy fought back as a member of the 4th RTR recalled :

Our objective was the high ground to the north-east of Sonsbeck – the last important high ground before the Rhine. Soon after 1400 hours the leading squadron moved into battle and a running fight started which lasted without a break until 0630 the next morning. At first the main local opposition came from German SPs, cunningly hidden. They took a lot of shifting and knocked out several tanks, killing a squadron leader amongst others, before they were knocked out in their turn. We took as our axis a road with a farm astride it every two or three hundred yards. Each farm was strongly defended by the Boche. We soon settled down into a set drill which each time ended in a mad rush by our infantry into the blazing buildings. The German gunners had a field day indeed. From their positions on the high ground they could see the movement of every tank and vehicle. Accurate and heavy fire took a distressingly large toll of our men, particularly of tank commanders who often had to be out of their tanks talking to the infantry. The steadiness and persistence of our infantry friends under this withering fire, and without the armoured protection we had, won our special admiration that day.

Hitler's military conferences at this time, the beginning of March, revealed at once his dissatisfaction with the way von Rundstedt – still Commander-in-Chief West, although not for much longer – was conducting the defence, how desperately short of troops and reserves he had become, and how all that was going wrong was the fault of others. Hitler did at least recognize the difficulties of making bricks without straw :

> Here on the Upper Rhine front something has to be made out of rubbish piles – the troops just aren't there. Commands are given in vain. [The Army Commander] can give orders to his two corps every day, and both of the corps can give them to their divisions, and the divisions can send the orders on down; but there is nothing there. . . .

When Jodl reported that von Rundstedt was waiting for a decision as to whether he would be authorized to consolidate his flanks, Hitler retorted that this merely meant that von Rundstedt wanted to retreat across the Rhine whereas Hitler required him to continue to defend further west :

> At any rate I want him to hang on to the West Wall as long as it is humanly possible. Above all we have to cure him of the idea of retreating here.* Because at the same moment the enemy will have the entire 6th English Army† and all the American troops free, and he'll throw them all in over here. These people just don't have any vision. That would just mean moving the catastrophe from one place to the other. The moment I move out of here, the enemy will have that whole army free. He [von Rundstedt] can't promise me that the enemy will stay here instead of going over here. There's no doubt that the building up of reserves at the most dangerous point here was not done with the energy that might have been possible. That wasn't so much Model's fault – he is concerned only with his own sector – that was the fault of the Commander-in-Chief West. . . .

*Hitler referred to the Maas sector on Montgomery's front.
†Hitler meant the British 2nd Army.

But the truth was that nothing the Commander-in-Chief West did could have withstood the weight and breadth of attack that Eisenhower's plans comprehended. On the same day that Simpson's 9th Army began its advance, Hodges 1st Army of Bradley's Army Group also crossed the Roer. He swept on quickly reaching Cologne on 5 March, while Patton with his customary dash crossed the south Eifel and advanced some 60 miles in three days reaching the junction of the Rhine and the Moselle on 7 March. Although bridge after bridge had been blown and gone crashing down into the river – some of them just as American tanks were racing up to reconnoitre and cross (one was even blown when American tanks were actually on it), wonder of wonders, something different occurred on 7 March. The leading formations of 9th Armoured Division spotted the railway bridge at Remagen – *intact*. The history of its capture and the fate of the local German commander (he was, of course, shot on Hitler's order) are well known. It was certainly touch and go. Small charges which detonated, main charges which did not, American engineers cutting every demolition cable they could see, tanks and infantry racing across the bridge, German attempts to lay further charges failing, a proper bridgehead established – it was a real-life case of the battle being lost for the want of a shoe nail.

At half-past ten on the morning of 7 March Lieutenant Larsen, an artillery observation pilot, saw that the bridge was intact. From then on the story moved forward with the terrible inevitability of a Jacobean tragedy. At roughly the same time as Captain Bratge, in charge of the bridge's close defensive garrison, was conferring with Major Scheller, Commander of the troops at Remagen (they were principally concerned with final preparations for demolition), leading elements of the American infantry and tank battalions directed on the bridge caught sight of it. When Brigadier General Hoge, commander of one of the combat teams of the 9th US Armoured Division, heard the news, he ordered his tanks and infantry to cross the bridge. Operations in war take a long time. It is one thing to give an order, another for those who have to execute it to receive the order, understand it, pass it on and actually see to it that the troops involved carry out their instructions. At a quarter past three in the afternoon Hoge had a message that the bridge was to be blown at 4 o'clock. He thereupon started bellowing further orders at his subordinates – smoke off the bridge with artillery, push tanks and infantry across, get the engineers to cut all the demolition wires. Even counter instructions from above (those above as usual had little notion either of what was happening at the front or what an opportunity was about to be seized or missed) did not dissuade Hoge. He was determined to get the bridge. Meanwhile Captain Bratge ordered Captain Friesenhahn, the German engineer technically responsible for demolition, to blow the bridge. But Friesenhahn remembered Hitler's former reminder that to blow the bridge prematurely would be as fatal to the man responsible as failure to blow it up at all. He insisted that Major Scheller – the tactical commander – give the order. Bratge persuaded Scheller to do so, and Friesenhahn turned the detonating device. It did not function – obviously American shelling had cut wires and put it out of action – so that he had to resort to the emergency charge. There was a great bang and for a moment both sides thought the bridge had gone. But the Americans soon saw it still standing, and across rushed the infantry. This was the beginning of the end for the German defenders. Bratge, who could not find Scheller, decided to fight no more. The American battalion of infantry was the first to cross and rapid repairs to the bridge allowed tanks to follow a few hours later. *Cross the Rhine with Dry Feet* – read the sign by us 9th Armoured Division. The price paid by Kesselring who on 10 March had taken over the Western front was that he was never able to contain or counter-attack the Remagen bridgehead, which by the same date was some 20,000 strong with more to come. The price paid by Scheller, and the others who were at the bridge, was death. Even the bridge's name was fitting for a drama of opportunities lost and won. It was that of another initial winner and ultimate loser whom power corrupted – Ludendorff.

There was no longer one more river to cross. The Americans were over it. There were many repercussions. Not only did the need to commit divisions at Remagen to ensure its retention affect the availability of forces for the three Army Groups involved in Eisenhower's three stage operation. Von Rundstedt was once more, and for the last time, relieved, and Kesselring, who had for so long and with such success held back the Allied armies in Italy, was appointed in his place.

The next stages in Allied operations were, of course, the assault crossing of the Rhine elsewhere. Bradley, who was all for exploiting tactical success and provided they were on his own front, brilliant at doing so, was seriously concerned not only that the Remagen windfall would not be properly followed up, but also that the demands of Montgomery's attack and advance in the north and Devers' in the south could only be met at his own expense, and that therefore his own part in the Rhine crossing and subsequent advance deep into Germany would not be the major one he so ardently desired. Patton who wholly sympathized with Bradley resorted to his normal recipe – of trying so to commit the American forces in their own sectors that there would be none to spare for exploiting Montgomery's successes if and when they transpired. But this was not Bradley's only cause of dissatisfaction – there was also the proposed use by Montgomery of 9th Army which properly belonged to him, Bradley. Montgomery's plan issued on 21 March for the crossing itself on 24 March, employed a US Corps under command of Dempsey's 2nd Army, but gave no role to HQ 9 US Army itself. There were good military reasons for not having too many cooks spoiling the broth on a relatively narrow frontage, but psychologically, particularly after the resentment caused by Montgomery's taking a good deal of credit for defeating the German Ardennes counter-offensive upon himself, it was a thoroughly bad move. Meanwhile the ruses conjured up by Patton and Bradley were paying big dividends, and the same day as Montgomery issued his plan, 21 March, Patton's 3rd Army racing through the Palatinate, had reached the west bank of the Rhine from Koblenz to Mannheim. Two days later on 23 March – and before Montgomery's attack started – Patton's men in the form of the 5th Infantry Division had actually crossed at Oppenheim, near Mainz, and established a bridgehead. Patton had 'bounced' the Rhine.

When Hitler heard this he commented on the respective dangers of the two bridgeheads, Remagen and Oppenheim, and even deluded himself that the crossing at Remagen was an advantage for them, in that it would be easier to contain two small groups, one at Oppenheim, which he considered the greater danger, and one at Remagen, than to deal with one crossing in strength in the south where more German troops might have been encircled. Even while he is discussing this point, Burgdorf* is badgering him with Goebbels' request to make the East-West Avenue in Berlin into an aircraft runway. Facing as he was the collapse of the Rhine defences, to say nothing of the Russians proximity both to Berlin and Vienna, the Führer fiddles about with details of chopping down lamp posts and part of the Tiergarten. A moment later he wants to know how Wenck is. He requires the doctor to commit himself definitely. 'I'll make him vouch for it with his head.' There was a lot of talk in these last days of people answering for this or that with their heads. Next when news comes in of Montgomery's

*General Burgdorf was Chief of Army Personnel Officer and Chief Adjutant of the Armed Forces.

assault across the Rhine either side of Wesel, Hitler begins to worry about five tank destroyers which are being repaired at Sennelager destined to help contain the Remagen bridgehead. When he hears they will not be ready until the next day 'then we'll take that up again tomorrow. If only we knew which of the 16 or 17 Tigers they brought back can be repaired, and when. That would be very important.' That Hitler who had formerly wielded Army Groups should be fussing about a few Tiger tanks and actually pretending or deceiving himself that they were important, that they could make any difference, shows us to what idiotic absurdities his conduct of war had degenerated. The only sensible remark he made at this conference was that there was too great a discrepancy between what the factories were supposed to be producing and what was being committed to the battle. There was an even greater discrepancy between what Hitler supposed was happening at the front and what really was. He had not seemed to grasp that there was now no fewer than three bridgeheads across the Third Reich's last great barrier in the West – at Wesel, Oppenheim and Remagen.

Although the Remagen bridgehead itself was not immediately exploited, its mere existence meant that Kesselring, Commander-in-Chief West, from 10 March, had to devote so many of his available forces to its containment that there was nothing he could do to prevent Patton's charge through the Palatinate. Kesselring's own comment was short and to the point :

> The gravest danger lay in the fact that Remagen required an increasing flow of reinforcements and by itself almost swallowed up the replacements and supplies fed to C-in-C West, magnetically attracting everything right and left. This made the regrouping, resting and refurbishing of the other Army Groups more difficult, if not impracticable. In fact, the first counter-measures against the first enemy forces to cross the Rhine had not been taken with the uncompromising fierceness which might have ensured a swift and relatively easy restoration of the line, and the fate of the whole Rhine front hung on our wiping out or containing the bridgehead.

In any event in the period between Montgomery's beginning his attacks on 8 February and Patton's crossing the Rhine at Oppenheim on 23 March, the command inherited by Kesselring was falling to pieces. Of approximately a million men committed to holding the West Wall, more than a third had gone – killed, wounded, or as the great bulk, nearly 300,000, were, made prisoners of war. Napoleon once boasted that he had an income of 100,000 soldiers a year, and had petulantly bellowed at Metternich that the loss of a million human beings meant nothing to a man like himself. Even though Hitler's income exceeded Napoleon's, he was spending it so prodigally, and had already used up so much of what replacements there were, that the whole cohesion of the Western front was bound to collapse before long. It was these ever widening signs of cracks in the wall which were the real vindication of Eisenhower's broad front strategy to which he had so persistently adhered.

It is a curious reflection on the different methods of supreme Command to note that, whereas the most skilful of Hitler's subordinates, like Model and Kesselring, would agree to anything the Führer proposed and then go their own way, Eisenhower would often seem to endorse his subordinates proposals and then continue with his own way. In any event it was clear that Eisenhower's overall strategy for the Rhineland battle, with the three parts we examined earlier, had succeeded brilliantly. Despite all the sceptics' doubts about dissipating his strength over so wide an area, his conduct of the battle was now paying great dividends. Field Marshal Sir Alan Brooke had been one of this plan's severest critics, but he was too honest and generous not to admit when he was wrong and he told Eisenhower how right he had been to stick to it. In a sense, although on a very different scale and in wholly different circumstances, the battle was a repetition of what had happened in North Africa and Normandy. The Allies with the very important advantage of overall superiority, and thus the ability to maintain balance by shifting their reserves and their main effort, had engaged the Germans in what amounted to a battle of attrition, had obliged them to commit their main strength in one area, so facilitating a breakthrough elsewhere. It was the old story. Given in a battle of this sort that there were no cardinal errors on either side, given too the determination to fight on in spite of heavy losses, it was bound to be the side able to afford and make good these losses which would win. But there was more to it than this. Bradley's tactical flair and improvization and Patton's drive and dash made certain that any opportunities which presented themselves would be fully exploited, and they were. This is to say nothing of the trump card the Allies still had in their hand – almost unlimited and unchallenged air power.

Montgomery, of course, did not operate like that. Improvization of a minor tactical nature, he endorsed. But the general concept, the master plan, which was always his own, had to conform to the basic rules of being tidy, elaborate, properly prepared and supported by massive fire power. Montgomery never really advanced in his tactical ideas beyond the First World War 'push'. The difference of *his* 'pushes' was that they succeeded. His push across the Rhine was no exception. On the night of 23 March, after the normal bombardment from thousands of guns, two British and two US infantry divisions crossed the river, either side of Wesel. Martin Lindsay and his 1st Battalion of Gordon Highlanders (whom we met before in the Reichswald) were among those who crossed the Rhine that night. The actual crossing was easy, but the subsequent fighting at Rees as unpleasant as any they had had:

It was a lovely night with a three-quarter moon. I shall always remember the scene in the loading area: the massive bulk of the buffaloes;* the long ghostly files of men marching up to them, their flickering shadows and those of a smashed farmhouse and the armoured car at the Royals' post; a few busy figures darting here and there in the moonlight directing people into this or that buffalo; a chink of light shining up from the slit entrance to the command post whence came a continued flow of radio conversation in the usual jargon. All this against the background of the guns firing with the steady rhythm of African drums.

War is full of contrasts, and just when the scene was looking at its most sinister and macabre, I saw something white scurry out of a hedge and dodge into a passing soldier ... it was a sheep and the first lamb of spring as they came trotting up the path towards me. ...

But the same enemy mortar was still smacking down right in the loading area, and I dreaded the thought of a mortar bomb landing in a buffalo with twenty-eight not-so-gay Gordons inside. However the battalion all got across the Rhine between 11.15 pm and 1 am, and without a single casualty – wonderful, wonderful luck.

During the battle for Rees it was a different story:

By the evening the enemy had been pushed back to quite a small area, about 200 yards by 200 yards, at the very east end of the town. B Company was trying to clean them up, as indeed they had been trying to do for the last three or four hours, while A and D Companies and the Black Watch to the north were acting as stops to prevent their breaking out. These Hun parachutists were very tough. They had been chased out of France, Belgium and Holland, into Germany, back over the Rhine, and now street by street across Rees into a corner. Yet they were still fighting it out. B Company had a

*A buffalo was an amphibious landing or river crossing craft.

very difficult fight and the two hours' work cost us three more officers ... The situation now was that the enemy were confined to the last hundred yards, at the very tip of the east end, but they were in a strong position with deep trenches and concrete and any attempts to get at it were met by heavy fire. I was going to make a last effort with C Company, when in came four or five prisoners, including a captain, who said he was in command ... He was marched in front of me as I sat at my table poring over the map, and gave me a spectacular Hitler salute which I ignored. I was very annoyed that, instead of being killed to a man, they had apparently won out in the end, escaping with their lives after shooting a lot of our chaps. He was a nasty piece of work, cocksure and good-looking in a flashy sort of way, but I had to admire the brave resistance which he had put up. The strain of battle was apparent in the dark black chasms under his eyes.

In addition to the assaulting formations two airborne divisions, one British, one US, had landed east of the river on 24 March. The great airborne Commander, General James Gavin, had a ringside seat to witness the operation and remembered in particular the number of aircraft set alight by German ground fire :

It was a new experience to fly an airborne mission but not jump it. It was an indescribably impressive sight. Three columns, each nine ships or double-tow gliders across, moved on the Rhine. On the far side of the river it was surprisingly dusty and hazy, no doubt caused by the earlier bombing and artillery fire. On the near bank of the Rhine clearly visible were panel letters to guide the troop-carrier pilots. Yellow smoke was also being used near the panels. It was hard to see how any pilot could make a serious navigational error. The air armada continued on and crossed the river. Immediately it was met by, what seemed to me, a terrific amount of flak. A number of ships and gliders went down in flames and after delivering their troops, a surprising number of troop-carrier pilots we saw on their way back were flying planes that were afire. The crew I was with counted twenty-three ships burning in sight at one time. But the in-coming pilots continued on their courses undeterred by the awesome spectacle ahead of them.

For once General Gavin was not taking part as his division was in reserve, but the men who parachuted had even more vivid memories.

One of the NCOs in C Company, 1st Royal Ulster Rifles, commanded by Major Huw Wheldon, was Staff Sergeant Cramer:

We were driven through the night to the airfield. All of us had a premonition. We had gone into D-Day light-hearted. But we had since been in the Ardennes, had seen what happened to other people, and were sure we were not coming back. There was a gloomy feeling. We had the Arnhem affair on our minds, as well, and it seemed hazardous, on the surface, crossing the Rhine. We had a fat-free breakfast and then I remember nothing until we were coming up to the Rhine – a glimmer through the smoke. Our smoke, German smoke, houses burning. Just a mass of smoke and flashes. We weren't aware of the AA, though it was there. Our glider was a Horsa carrying C Company HQ – Major Wheldon, myself, five rifle-men, a trailer with stores and ammo, and two very upset parachutists (their first glider lift). As we went over the Rhine, there was a lot of shouting up front, in the cockpit, something obviously wrong there. I don't know if we were cast off, or if we cast off, but we were going down at the rate of knots. We levelled out – terrified! – then there was a terrific crash, something broke open the floor of the glider and a spray of fine earth came in. Wheldon was yelling, 'Get out! get out quick!' for this was the vulnerable moment, but the door was jammed and had to be forced open. Fortunately we had landed in a kind of hollow, which was dead ground, and skimming just over us was 20-mm tracer. We ran to the nearest line of hedges, and I confess we were in so much of a hurry that I had to go back for my Sten. . . . The noise of SA fire, mortar fire and artillery was increasing all the time. We saw many American dead and wounded. It appeared that the American infantrymen were not trained in 'battle noises.' They seemed to drop to the ground and fire, whenever shots were heard close by. When passing a burning farmhouse, there was a sound of what appeared to be a machine-gun; no one could have been in the house, because of the flames, and it was obviously ammunition burning; but it took some time to get the Americans up and on again. As we got to the LZ, I saw a figure in a long German greatcoat rise to his feet from the centre of a field, and walk towards us with his hands up. The man was Volkssturm, about 50 or 60 years of age, a long, thin chap. Before we could do anything about it, three Americans let fly with their carbines and the figure fell. God, we were angry. So was Major Wheldon. . . . Back at Battalion, I was shocked by the casualties (16 officers, 243 other ranks). But the Typhoons, my God they were good. We were very jumpy, from our heavy losses and having no ground troops near. Then the Tiffies appeared and sorted out the enemy armour. They operated only two or three hundred yards in front of you. When we advanced later, we saw the terrible damage they had done; the Germans were terrified of them. In a field in front of us, between the two armies, a light observation plane came down smack. The Germans fired at it and we fired at them. We saw the door open and a young American officer come out. He ran the hundred yards in four seconds, to a roar of cheering from us. But there was a sad affair during the landing. Sergeant Major McCutchan, M.M. was caught in the centre of the road by a German tank. He couldn't get away, so he went on firing at the tank until it hit him and ran over him. I had his rifle afterwards, you couldn't get the bloodstains off. There was a horrible sight in a field nearby – a wounded American with the flesh of his chest torn away and all the rib cage exposed. One thing I did notice. The Americans will bunch, whereas we go up two sides of a road. It was purely a matter of lack of experience. They were shouting at each other and firing at nothing. They're still doing it in Vietnam. There was a film of them at place called Hue, and it was just the same. One thing I'll say for the Germans; they were better than we were with enemy dead; buried them properly and neatly with their equipment (which had their numbers on) over the crosses.

The Allies were still a long way from Berlin, although one of the RAF pilots towing gliders found that his particular glider was so long in casting off that he wondered if its crew had decided to go on to Berlin and if so felt himself obliged to try and get them there. But eventually the glider did cast off. The whole operation was costly, but effective, for since the German defenders had only about five divisions spread over a 30 miles front between Emmerich and the Ruhr, it was hardly surprising that Montgomery very rapidly not merely established a bridgehead but broke out again from it. The restraints imposed on his advance were more those of bridges, routes and logistics than of the enemy. A week after crossing the Rhine, Montgomery had 20 divisions* and 1,500 tanks under his hand to advance – first to provide the northern part of a pincer to encircle the Ruhr, then to gallop across the Westphalian plain to the Elbe.

*At this point Montgomery still had the 1st Canadian, 2nd British and 9th US Armies under his command.

Meanwhile Eisenhower instructed Bradley, suitably reinforced by more American divisions, to complete the Ruhr encirclement and drive east to link up with the Red Army. Accordingly on 28 March Hodges' 1st Army broke out of the greatly stronger and wider Remagen bridge-head – it extended roughly from Bonn to Koblenz – in an eastern direction, while Patton's 3rd Army advanced from the Mainz area. Three days later Patton and Hodges joined hands near Giessen, and breaking clear of Kesselring's delaying forces thrust on to the Frankfurt-Kassel area in order to close the trap east of Model's Army Group which was defending the Ruhr. There was a major tank battle at Sennelager – the famous panzer training area – but the comparatively few tanks and SP guns the Germans had mustered could not prevail against the numbers enjoyed by the Americans. Model was surrounded and with him over 300,000 men. Model himself preferred suicide to capture.

It was a comparable choice which seemed to face another German commander – the Supreme Commander of the Wehrmacht, Hitler himself. For as March 1945 came to a close, he was faced with some disagreeable military realities, which would require all his will power and all his gift for reducing problems to their simplest terms. The facts were that since the turn of the year everything had gone wrong. Attack in the West had failed with the costly Ardennes offensive and now defence in the West had failed too. Eisenhower's armies were across the Rhine and there seemed little to stop them motoring on to the Elbe and beyond. Attack in the East had also failed with the abortive Danube offensive and the futile attempts to savage Zhukov's northern flank. Defence in the East had failed as well and the Red Army was across the Oder, on the Elbe and within a few days' march of Berlin. This one place alone remained to him, the Bunker beneath the Reich Chancellory, last of the Führer headquarters. Here he would now 'direct' the final and conclusive battle of the war – the battle for Berlin itself. Here the turning point would come and he would inflict the greatest of defeats on the enemy that had done him so much damage – the Russians. He would, like Frederick the Great and Mr Micawber, wait for something to turn up, and if nothing did turn up then, as those two had threatened but not actually done, there was always the bare bodkin. He would make Berlin his everlasting mansion while he built his ship of death for the longest journey over the last of seas.

8

WHO IS TO HAVE BERLIN?

I say quite frankly that Berlin remains of high strategic importance ...should [it] be in our grasp we should certainly take it.

CHURCHILL to ROOSEVELT, 1 April 1945

If there were one man on the Allied side who more than any other influenced the decision not to go all out for Berlin, that man was Eisenhower. For, as is (and always will be) the custom with military commanders, he changed his mind. On 15 September 1944, after the great victory in Normandy, he had addressed a letter to his two principal subordinates, Bradley and Montgomery, in which he outlined his views as to future operations and asked for theirs. At this time it was clear from his letter that he regarded Berlin as a primary objective. Assuming as he did that before long (it was to be longer than he supposed) the Ruhr, the Saar and Frankfurt would be in their hands, he went on: 'Clearly, Berlin is the main prize. ... There is no doubt whatsoever, in my mind, that we should concentrate all our energies and resources on a rapid thrust to Berlin. Our strategy, however, will have to be coordinated with that of the Russians. ...' He added that precise objectives could not be defined until nearer the time.

This was itself a questionable assumption, for, while never losing sight of opportunism, it is always sounder to know what it is you want to do and decide how to do it than not to know and not to decide. It is always better to lay down objectives which will then determine the shape of operations rather than loosely allow the way operations develop to determine which objectives you will go for. Yet Eisenhower did no more than foresee a series of alternative moves for which they must be prepared. Among them was one in which the Russians might 'beat us to Berlin'. The alternatives were to thrust along the axis Ruhr-Hanover-Berlin or Frankfurt-Leipzig-Berlin or both. If the Russians did get to Berlin first, then Montgomery's northern group of armies would go for Hanover and Hamburg, while Bradley's central group would aim at Leipzig-Dresden. In either case Devers' southern group of armies would seize the area Augsberg-Munich. 'Simply stated,' the letter concluded, 'it is my desire to move on Berlin by the most direct and expeditious route, with combined us-British forces supported by other available forces moving through key centres and occupying strategic areas on the flanks, all in one coordinated, concerted operation.' Cutting out the verbiage and allowing for loose wording, the message was clear. Berlin was the goal. While not agreeing with much else in Eisenhower's letter, in his answer to it Montgomery put his finger firmly on this point and urged the Supreme Commander to decide there and then what was necessary to go to Berlin 'and finish the war; the remainder must play a secondary role.' Therefore, Montgomery argued, the plan and objectives had to be agreed at once and could not wait until nearer the time.

The trouble was that there was no absolutely clear and clearly understood policy. The British all along had not only seen Berlin as the goal of the Allied forces (as indeed it was defined by Supreme Headquarters in May 1944 before Operation *Overlord* actually started) but also had always been convinced that it was to be their own principal contribution to these forces – 21st Army Group under Montgomery – which would make the main thrust in the north. But at no time had the Combined Chiefs of Staff laid down in unequivocal terms what Eisenhower was to do after crossing the Rhine. Indeed in spite of all his previous references to Berlin, Eisenhower's strategy had consistently been to advance on a broad front with primary and secondary thrusts, and then as he told Marshall, us Army Chief of Staff, having linked up the two advancing forces in the general area of Kassel, 'make one great thrust to the eastward'. But where to? That was the point. Lack of decision here meant that on actually crossing the Rhine and moving eastward, the aim of the Allied armies was far from clear. Also to be remembered was that whatever objectives the Allies cared to choose were probably realizable, for the German forces in the West (now under Field Marshal Kesselring who had relieved von Rundstedt on 10 March) could no longer fight a coordinated and successful defensive battle however determined the resistance of individual parts of the front might be. Nominally there might still be 65 German divisions on the Western front. For practicable purposes there were small battle groups, divisional staffs, survivors of former battles. All of them were dispersed and without proper communications or logistic support. The

Red Army artillery opens fire on Berlin

Red Army in Berlin

Red Army in Berlin

German prisoners of war

Allied will, whatever it might be, could not be thwarted by such relics of the formerly all-powerful Wehrmacht.

Eisenhower's broad plan for the encirclement of the Ruhr was that forces of Montgomery's 21st Army Group, specifically the US 9th Army under his command, would break out of their bridgehead over the Rhine north of the Ruhr, thrust along the northern part of the Ruhr and link up with the US 1st Army, from Bradley's 12th Army Group, which would break out from the extended Remagen bridgehead. After this junction, the whole area east of the Rhine would be occupied and the further advance into Germany would get under way.

Montgomery was quite clear as to what he intended to do once the junction had been effected, and on 27 March issued his orders accordingly, at the same time informing both Eisenhower and the CIGS, Sir Alan Brooke. These orders were in essence that the 2nd British and 9th US Armies should advance with maximum speed and energy to the Elbe from Hamburg to Magdeburg, while 1st Canadian Army cleared Holland. Great emphasis was made of the need to 'get the whips out' and lead the advance with fast moving armoured spearheads, capturing airfields on the way to ensure their subsequent use for close air support. But the following day, when Montgomery's troops had already begun their advance, came the bombshell. Eisenhower not only completely changed the plan but communicated directly with Stalin in order to coordinate his operations with those of the Red Army. His signal to Montgomery endorsed the latter's plan only up to the point of his linking up with Bradley east of the Ruhr. Thereafter it not only removed the 9th US Army from Montgomery's command, but made it plain that the main Allied thrust would be, not to Berlin, but to Leipzig and Dresden.

As soon as you and Bradley have joined hands in the Kassel-Paderborn area Ninth Army will revert to Bradley's command.* He will then be responsible for occupying and mopping up the Ruhr and with minimum delay will make his main thrust on the axis Erfurt-Leipzig-Dresden and join hands with the Russians.

Meanwhile Montgomery's Army Group was to protect Bradley's northern flank while continuing to advance to the Elbe in the north. Devers would protect Bradley's southern flank and when possible advance to link up with the Russians in the Danube basin. When Montgomery made an appeal to him not to change either the plan or

---

*In addition Bradley was given the newly arrived US 15th Army.

H

the command arrangements until the Elbe had been reached, Eisenhower signalled his intentions more fully :

> My plan is simple, it aims at dividing and destroying the enemy
> forces and joining hands with the Russian Army. Subject to any
> information which Stalin may give me, the axis Kassel-Leipzig
> appears the most direct line of advance for achieving this object.

After attaining his Leipzig objective Eisenhower saw his main strength
poised in that area ready to go north to seize naval or political objectives or south in case the Germans should succeed in creating any
concentration of forces there. Adaptability was all. Yet there was, it
will be noted, no mention of going east. Since before this move to
Leipzig, Bradley would be responsible for establishing control of the
Ruhr, he must have the US 9th Army to enable him to do so.
Therefore Eisenhower reiterated his decision to remove this Army from
Montgomery after the junction of the two Army Groups at Paderborn,
but he promised to give Montgomery 24 hours notice before it was
withdrawn. He went on :

> You will see that in none of this do I mention Berlin. So far as I am
> concerned, that place has become nothing but a geographical loca-
> tion; I have never been interested in those. My purpose is to destroy
> the enemy forces and his power to resist.

At this point we might well ask not merely why Eisenhower changed
his mind but in what way he had changed it. For that he had done so is
not in doubt. The change lay in his conception of Berlin as a military
and political objective. In spite of his previous emphasis that Berlin was
the main prize, and that above all the Allies should concentrate everything on a rapid thrust there no matter how this was to be done, in spite
also of his iteration that all his plans boiled down in the end to exactly
this – 'to move on Berlin by the most direct and expeditious route' – he
now dismissed the city as a mere geographical location. Why? It is easy
enough to understand that he should regard the capture of Berlin as no
longer feasible – after all as 21st Army Group was ready to break out
from the Rhine bridgehead, it was still 300 miles from Berlin, while the
Russians, already across the Oder, were less than 40 miles from the
city. Indeed he had already foreseen losing the race to Berlin in his 15
September letter, and in that event Montgomery was to go for
Hanover and Hamburg, while Bradley aimed at Leipzig and Dresden.
In this respect therefore he was simply putting into practice a foreseen
contingency plan. But this in itself did not alter Berlin's importance. It

s also easy to understand Eisenhower's concern that Model's Army Group in the Ruhr should be properly dealt with so that there could be no question of the Germans re-establishing a coherent defensive front in the central area. It is even easy to understand, although not to endorse, Eisenhower's worries about the possibilities of Hitler's retiring to the so-called 'National Redoubt' in the Bavarian and Austrian mountains and conducting there a last desperate stand which might take much time and many lives to reduce. All this can be understood. What is not so easy to understand in view of Eisenhower's insistence on the whole purpose of military operations being in pursuit of political aims and the undisputed importance of Berlin as a political objective, is that he should have suddenly turned fully 180 degrees about and pronounced it to be of no significance. And the supreme irony of it all in view of Eisenhower's reiteration that what he was after was the destruction of the enemy's will to resist is that Berlin up to the very last, leaving aside its weight in the political game, contained the one military objective without whose seizure or démise the enemy's will to resist would never be broken and the war would never end – the person of Adolf Hitler himself. Nor is it easy to understand why Eisenhower should have chucked away the possibility of taking Berlin with his own armies before it had become plain that he could not do it.

Eisenhower's change of mind was predictably as acceptable to Stalin as it was unacceptable to Churchill. Eisenhower's signal to the Russian leader, sent on 28 March, with information copies to Combined Chiefs of Staff and the British Chiefs of Staff was as follows :

1. My immediate operations are designed to encircle and destroy the enemy forces defending the Ruhr and to isolate that area from the rest of Germany. This will be accomplished by developing around north of Ruhr and from Frankfurt through Kassel line until I close the ring. The enemy thus encircled will then be mopped up.

2. I estimate that this phase of the operation will end late in April or even earlier, and my next task will be to divide the remaining enemy forces by joining hands with your forces.

3. For my forces the best axis on which to effect this junction would be Erfurt-Leipzig-Dresden. I believe, moreover, that this is the area to which main German Governmental Departments are being moved. It is along this axis that I propose to make my main effort. In addition, as soon as the situation allows, a secondary advance will be made to effect a junction with your forces in the area Regensburg-

Linz, thereby preventing the consolidation of German resistance in Redoubt in Southern Germany.

Eisenhower concluded his message by asking what Russian intentions were so that properly coordinated action as to direction and timing between the two sides could be effected and by offering liaison officers to perfect this coordination. The pleasure with which Eisenhower's message was received by Stalin was in sharp contrast to reactions in London. Stalin's reply on 1 April agreed in principle and in detail to what Eisenhower had proposed – except for the sending of liaison officers. Stalin made four memorable points in his telegram – first that the Red Army and the Western Allies forces should join up in the area Erfurt, Leipzig, Dresden; secondly 'Berlin has lost its former strategic importance. In the Soviet High Command plans, secondary forces will therefore be allotted in the direction of Berlin';* thirdly that the main blow by Soviet forces would begin in approximately the second half of May;† lastly that the Germans were reinforcing the Eastern front with the 6th ss Panzer Army together with three divisions from Italy and two from Norway. Immediately following receipt of Stalin's reply Eisenhower issued the orders to give effect to his plan.

Meanwhile there was consternation in London not only because of what Eisenhower's plans were, but because of his method of communicating them directly to Stalin. The British Chiefs of Staff considered that in doing this he had usurped the authority and responsibility of Roosevelt, Churchill, their governments and their combined military advisers. Furthermore to the British military men, the plan itself was faulty. We have seen already what it was that influenced Eisenhower's decision – his acknowledgement of the fact that the Russians with the best part of a million soldiers were so close to Berlin, his obsession with the need to overwhelm and put out of action Model's Army Group, and his fear about a Nazi stronghold in the south. To the British Eisenhower's reasoning was neither clear nor satisfactory. In the first place the dangers of a National Redoubt in Bavaria were regarded by the British as something of a myth. Nor could they take their eyes off what to them was the much more important north – with the Baltic and North Sea ports to think of, prevention of any further U-boat offensives and the liberation of Denmark and Norway. So they

---

*Churchill's subsequent comment was: 'This statement was not borne out by events'.

†It began a month earlier – on 16 April.

emained unconvinced and voiced their objections in a signal to Washington.

It took their own Prime Minister to put them right both as to procedural and strategic realities. Whatever the British Chiefs of Staff might say and think, it had to be remembered that Eisenhower's prestige in Washington was extremely high. He had crossed the Rhine, created the options of advancing in the north, centre and south, and had in American eyes earned 'a right and indeed a vital need, to try to elicit from the Russians their views as to the best point for making contact by the armies of the West and of the East'. Churchill dismissed his military advisers' concern about Denmark and Norway as contradicting the prime necessity of destroying the main enemy forces and advancing to Berlin. The Prime Minister's own apprehensions were of a very different sort, and, as we have seen in the first chapter, he criticized Eisenhower's plan because it shifted the axis of advance. To Churchill it was not merely that momentum in driving on Berlin must be maintained – and maintained incidentally by British forces – but that Berlin must fall quickly and with its fall bring down what German hopes might still survive.

As usual when it came to big issues, Churchill's strategic instinct did not forsake him. In this instance it embraced not merely the final stages of one great struggle, but the beginnings of another, for already the behaviour of the Russians in going back on principles agreed at Yalta was causing him grave concern as to Russian policy. He had to be cruel, only to be kind, to be firm at the present time in order to have some chance of safeguarding the future. In accordance with these ideas Churchill was anxious that the Allied Armies should do all they could to put the West in the best possible position for subsequent confrontations with the Russians if they came. He told Roosevelt he was in no doubt that the rapid advances by their armies had both surprised and displeased the Russian leaders and that their armies should meet the Russian armies as far east as they could, and if possible should enter Berlin. But Roosevelt was dying and Marshall who supported his protégé Eisenhower through thick and thin, as did the American Joint Chiefs of Staff, endorsed both the plans he had made and his action in communicating those plans to the Russians. Nonetheless Eisenhower was asked to elaborate. This he did on 31 March. In a message to Churchill on the following day he explained that he had not changed his plan, which had always been to concentrate his forces east of the Rhine in the general area of Kassel and then determine which direction the next blow or blows aimed at further disrupting the German power

to resist would take. He had, he claimed, never lost sight of the drive t
the north. He insisted that at that particular time the central concer
tration was essential to his strategy. On the same day Churchill sent
telegraph to Roosevelt in which he attempted to summarize his mi:
givings and his differences with Eisenhower. These differences, h
explained, were of emphasis, not of principle. But up to now the ax:
had been to Berlin. Eisenhower wished to shift it further south throug.
Leipzig to Dresden. To do this 9th us Army would quit 21st Arm
Group and so rob it of the strength to push beyond the Elbe. Berli
remained of high strategic importance. 'Nothing will exert a psychc
logical effect of despair upon all German forces or resistance equal t
that of the fall of Berlin – on the other hand, if left to itself to maintai
a siege by the Russians among its ruins and as long as the German Fla;
flies there, it will animate the resistance of all Germans under arms.
Besides the Russians were bound to capture Vienna. Were they to b
allowed to capture Berlin too? If Berlin were within the Western armie
grasp, Churchill concluded, they should take it.

Meanwhile, and still on the same day, 1 April 1945, Stalin wa
conducting a conference in Moscow at which Zhukov and Konev
respectively commanders of the 1st Belorussian and 1st Ukrainia:
fronts, and Antonev and Shtemenko, both of the General staff, wer
present. Stalin asked Shtemenko to read out a telegram which gave th
rather surprising information that the Anglo/American command wa
getting ready to launch an operation to capture Berlin, with the mai
forces for it under Montgomery's command. The axis would be north
of the Ruhr, which was the shortest route for the Allied forces, and th
telegram (we cannot help wondering whether it was simply a bad piec
of intelligence or one fabricated by Stalin) finished by saying that th
Allied preparations and plans were such that they would certainl
reach Berlin before the Red Army. Stalin then asked his two com
manders: 'Who is going to take Berlin, we or the Allies?' Konev replie
at once that the Soviets would take Berlin, and more particularly hi
own *front,* even though this would mean a good deal of redeployment
Zhukov went one better and pointed out that his *front* was poised an
ready now to take Berlin and what is more it was nearest to the city
Stalin, always ready to aggravate the rivalry of these two men, ordere
them to prepare their proposals at once while still in Moscow so that i
a day or so they could return to their commands with approved plan
in their hands. Two days later Stalin listened to their ideas. Each pu
his own claim forward, and to resolve their differences Stalin drew a
line on a map between the two *fronts.* The line ran roughly from just

south of Gubin on the river Neisse to Lübben on the river Spree. 'Who ever gets there first', declared Stalin, 'will also take Berlin.' The Russian General Staff itself had all along favoured a grand pincer movement to encircle and attack the city and this in the end is what took place. Zhukov's subsequent record of this meeting makes the point that in fact his own *front* was charged with the direct advance on the city and its seizure, while Konev's front was to attack across the Neisse and prevent the German Army Group Centre from interfering. In other words Konev was to operate in support of Zhukov. At the same time Zhukov concedes that Stalin did add that if his own 1st Belorussian *front* should be held up to the east of Berlin, Konev's 1st Ukrainian *front* would be ready to attack Berlin from the south.

Thus during the first week of April 1945 we have two Russian Army Group commanders preparing and perfecting their plans to take Berlin. At the same time to balance the British pressures, Eisenhower was being strongly supported by his own countrymen. Bradley had produced the most extraordinary estimate that to advance from the Elbe to Berlin would cost the Western Allies 100,000 casualties which he thought 'a pretty stiff price to pay for a prestige objective.' Such an estimate, as we shall see, was hardly supportable by examining military facts, but Bradley could not but be unaware that a drive on Berlin, in view of the deployment of his and Montgomery's Army Groups, could hardly be done by his own men. 'We were less concerned', wrote Bradley later, 'with postwar political alignments than destruction of what remained of the German Army. . . . As soldiers we looked naively on this British inclination to complicate the war with political foresight and non military objectives.' Naive is the right word. For what are military operations but the determination of political circumstances? What are political circumstances but the illustration of military operations?

Be that as it may, Bradley's influence was further reinforced by Marshall's. Speaking for the US Chiefs of Staff, Marshall laid down that quick and complete victory was their sole objective and that such psychological and political advantages as would result from the possible capture of Berlin ahead of the Russians should not override the imperative military consideration which, 'in our opinion, is the destruction and dismemberment of the German armed forces.' The victory of the North in the war between the States – notable example of military success and political failure – has much to answer for. The recipient of all this advice, Eisenhower, still kept the options open, and despite having issued his orders in accordance with his own previous decisions, had not absolutely closed his mind to other possibilities. On 7 April he signalled to Marshall that there would be no drive on Berlin until he had joined forces with the Russians in the centre, reached the Baltic and overrun the National Redoubt. Yet:

> I am the first to admit that a war is waged in pursuance of political aims, and if the Combined Chiefs of Staff should decide that the Allied effort to take Berlin outweighs military considerations in this theatre, I would cheerfully readjust my plans. . . .

He was not required to do so. This made it certain that the Russians would have Berlin and we shall see later how they went about it. What may still be worth asking is – if the Combined Chiefs of Staff had decided on 7 April in response to Eisenhower's offer to go then and there for Berlin with all the strength he could muster, could he have got there first? The very next day, 8 April, we find Eisenhower telling Montgomery: 'if I get an opportunity to capture Berlin cheaply, I will take it'. Even Bradley, finding three days later that his armies had secured a bridgehead over the Elbe at Magdeburg and were only 50 miles from Berlin, admitted: 'At that time we could probably have pushed on to Berlin had we been willing to take the casualties Berlin would have cost us. Zhukov had not yet crossed the Oder* and Berlin now lay about midway between our forces.'

Chester Wilmot was in no doubt on the matter. He pointed out that there were no prepared defences to prevent Eisenhower reaching Berlin first, no unbreakable obstacles, 'nor any resistance that could not be brusquely swept aside by the 60 divisions available for his next offensive'. What is more, Wilmot argued, there were no logistic objections either. Unlike the situation in the Autumn of 1944 when the great breakout from Normandy, with Antwerp still not cleared, outran administrative resources, in the spring of 1945 there were no logistic reasons for not carrying the Allied armies to Berlin in overwhelming numbers. 'Politically, too, the way was clear for, though the German capital lay in the centre of that area which was to be occupied by the Soviet Union after the war, it had never been suggested that the military forces of one power should not enter the occupation zone of another in pursuit of the common enemy.' Indeed at no time had there been any discussion between the Soviet Union and the Western Allies as to who was to take Berlin. At Yalta the question did not arise; certainly there was no agreement that the city was to be reserved for

---

*Bradley was referring not to footholds but the proper Russian attack across the Oder, which did not take place for another five days – on 16 April.

the Red Army. Since Yalta, of course, the circumstances which had been so agreeable to Stalin – his own armies everywhere advancing, his Allies' armies bogged down – had been totally reversed. Freedom of movement had returned to Eisenhower and it was the Red Army which had been halted. It is perhaps by glancing at what happened in the final April battles, therefore, that the point as to whether the Western armies could or could not have got to Berlin first may finally be resolved. In resolving it we must ask too whether the German commanders in the field – notwithstanding anything the Führer or okw might have had to say – would have allowed the Western armies to make their way to and into the capital. Leaving aside resistance by fanatical and scattered groups, if a decision of this sort had been left to such men as Guderian, Wenck, Busse, Kesselring, von Manteuffel, Heinrici, Speer, Dönitz, even Jodl and Himmler, the answer would almost certainly have been 'Yes'.

9

FIVE MINUTES PAST TWELVE

My Führer, I congratulate you! Roosevelt is dead. It is written in the stars that the second half of April will be the turning-point for us. This is Friday, April the 13th. It is the turning point.

GOEBBELS to HITLER

What was happening on Friday 13 April? Inside the Bunker where Hitler presided over the almost extinct relics of power it might seem to be an auspicious day. Outside it was a different matter. What though Roosevelt were dead; the armies of which he had been Commander-in-Chief were not. Nor were those of Churchill or Stalin. What exactly were they up to?

We have seen that General Eisenhower's broad plan was to close up to the Elbe with several things in mind – to link up with the Russians in the area Leipzig-Dresden, further to link up in the south and to prevent the establishment of a National Redoubt, and to cross the Elbe in the north in order to drive to the Baltic coast. On 10 April Bradley and Montgomery conferred at the latter's headquarters. Both Army Group commanders made it clear that they were going to push on to the Elbe, Montgomery with Dempsey's 2nd Army, Bradley with 1st and 9th US Armies. Opposing the advancing Allies and roughly defending the front between Bremen and Magdeburg was a reorganized German command. Student's 1st Parachute Army and Blumentritt's Army were responsible to an Army Group headquarters under Field Marshal Busch which would coordinate the operations of these two armies and also Blaskowitz's forces in Holland.

The British 2nd Army's operations in spite of hard fighting particularly at the many rivers were swift and successful. They captured Celle on 12 April, Uelzen was reached on 15 April. The notorious Belsen concentration camp was revealed in all the horror of its 40,000 living but starved men, women and children, its 10,000 unburied dead lying about the place, the pits with further untold thousands of decomposing bodies. Typhus and typhoid stalked everywhere. The British then turned north to reach the Elbe in the Hamburg-Darchau area. Lüneburg was taken on 18 April but the intact railway bridge over the Elbe at Lauenburg was blown up by the Germans on the next day before the 11th Armoured Division could reach it. Further west Verden was captured on 17 April and two days later the famous Desert Rats, 7th Armoured Division, were a few miles from Hamburg. Hamburg was not occupied until some two weeks later and then without a fight. We may perhaps anticipate its occupation with a glance at what Richard Brett-Smith, at the time a young officer in the armoured car regiment of 7th Armoured Division, the 11th Hussars, had to say about it, and the surrendering German Army:

> We did not know, when we waited on our armoured cars that afternoon of 3 May 1945, ready to enter Hamburg, whether we would have to fight our way up Schleswig-Holstein and into Denmark. Naturally we hoped that we would not have to. . . .
>
> When it was nearly seven o'clock in the evening, we led the Division through Harburg and over the Elbe into Hamburg itself. . . . There was something unnatural about the silence, something a little uncanny. As we drove up to that last great bridge across the Elbe, the final obstacle that could have held us up so long, it seemed impossible that we had taken Hamburg so easily. Looking down at the cold grey waters of the Elbe swirling far below, we sensed again that queer feeling that came whenever we crossed an enemy bridge, and it would have been no great surprise if the whole structure had suddenly collapsed. . . . But no, it did not blow up . . . we were across the last obstacle, and there were no more rivers to cross. . . . There was a lot of clicking of heels and saluting, and in a few moments Hamburg, the greatest port of Germany had been surrendered. . . .
>
> The end of the German Army was indeed a wonderful and astonishing sight. We had long guessed how disorganized the enemy was, and that his administration had broken down, but even so, the sight we now saw was stranger than we had ever expected. Thousands of infantry, *Luftwaffe* men, ss men, anti-tank gunners, *Kriegsmarinen,* Hungarians, Rumanians, ambulance men, Labour Corps men, *Hitler Jugend* boys, soldiers of every conceivable age and unit,

jostled one another in complete disorder ... down every road the *Wehrmacht* struggled to give itself up, its pride broken, its endurance at an end. ... The Army Group of Field Marshal Busch was anxious for two things only – the safety of a British prison cage, and food. ...

All this was still to come, but during the first weeks of April Dempsey's 2nd Army had advanced some 200 miles and was, as Montgomery and Eisenhower had intended, on the Elbe. Meanwhile the 1st Canadian Army had been clearing Holland. Now came further tasks for Montgomery's Army Group – to cross the Elbe seize Wismar, Lübeck, clear Schleswig Holstein, take Emden, Wilhelmshaven and Cuxhaven, and capture Bremen. For all this Montgomery did not have sufficient strength and Eisenhower allotted him XVIII US Airborne Corps. These additional troops enabled Montgomery to fulfil his mission – and the first British and Russian contact was made on 2 May near Wismar. We may suppose therefore that *given these tasks*, any idea that Montgomery's Army Group could have reached Berlin before the Russians is absurd. What about the Americans and Bradley's Army Group – could they have done so?

On 1 April the 1st and 9th US Armies had effected their planned junction at Lippstadt west of Paderborn. At this point, it will be remembered, 9th Army was to leave Montgomery's command and revert to Bradley's, so that the latter could both control the Ruhr and push on east to Leipzig and Dresden. Eisenhower's directive of 2 April laid down what the American armies were then to do. His broad intention was still to divide and destroy the German forces by thrusting forward on the axis Kassel-Leipzig and there meet and join up with the Red Army. Bradley's specific tasks were to mop up the Ruhr pocket, and advance to the Elbe astride Eisenhower's main axis, Kassel-Leipzig, with from north to south 9th Army directed roughly at Tangemünde and Magdeburg; 1st Army at Wittenberg and Leipzig; 3rd Army at Bayreuth. On reaching the Elbe the American 1st and 9th Armies were to establish bridgeheads and be prepared to continue the advance. Meanwhile 6th Army Group would protect the southern flank and make for Nuremberg-Regensburg-Linz to prevent the Germans from establishing any properly coordinated defence in the south. That Bradley's operations to the east and south east were so successful was due in large measure to his early elimination of Model's group of armies in the Ruhr encirclement. In this operation no fewer than eighteen divisions of the 15th, 1st and 9th US Armies were

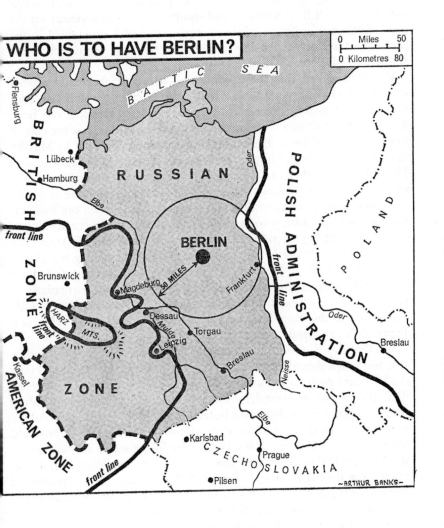

involved, attacking from all sides, and in spite of some fanatical resistance at a few points and in spite of all Hitler's orders about no surrender, by 10 April the Germans were surrendering in droves. On 18 April the thing was over. A total of 320,000 soldiers were taken together with all their weapons and equipment. It was a victory on the scale of the end in North Africa. A huge gap had been created in the centre of Germany's defences and it left the way largely clear for Bradley to advance.

Eisenhower had long been concerned to avoid accidental clashes with the Red Army and so had laid down a line at which Bradley's forces should stop before receiving further orders. This line ran from Bayreuth to Chemnitz and then along the river Mulde, passing east of Leipzig, to the Elbe at Dessau and thence along the Elbe to Magdeburg and Wittenberg. Simpson's 9th US Army reached the Elbe astride Magdeburg as early as 11 April and by the next day were across it. On the same day Tangemünde was reached – and Tangemünde was only just more than 50 miles from Berlin – this at a time when the Russians were still on the Oder, some 40 miles from Berlin, and were not due to start their next big offensive for another four days – on 16 April. The US 1st Army too under Hodges got on very quickly reaching the Mulde on 15 April, although Halle and Leipzig were still holding out. Patton's 3rd Army, as might have been expected from the man, particularly as he had least opposition in front of him, got on furthest and fastest of all, and reached the stop line west of Chemnitz at Plauen, Hof and Bayreuth by 15 April.

On that day Simpson, commanding 9th Army, proposed to Bradley that his troops should expand the bridgehead they had established over the Elbe and push on in force for Berlin. Eisenhower vetoed the suggestion. We cannot but wonder what would have happened had Patton been commanding in this sector instead of Simpson. Patton presumably would have acted first and asked permission later. That Simpson could have got on seems more or less certain for in the whole advance up to the Elbe he had suffered very few casualties and opposing him at this point were mainly scattered, ill-equipped and unpractised divisions of Wenck's 12th Army* which had no air support at all. But this would have meant a fundamental change of heart on the part of the Supreme Commander. The day before Simpson's proposal Eisenhower had indicated to the Combined Chiefs of Staff that the essence of his plan was

---

*Wenck's own comment was: 'If the Americans launch a major attack they'll crack our positions with ease. After all what's to stop them? There's nothing between here and Berlin.'

to halt and make a firm front on the Elbe and tidy up the flanks – the
tidying up to include advancing to the Baltic and to Denmark in the
north and in the south to join up with the Rusisans in the Danube
valley in order to destroy the Redoubt if it existed. As any idea of
thrusting on Berlin would in his view have to await the outcome of
these other operations, he did not propose to incorporate it in his plans
at that time. He made it clear to Marshall that he regarded the Baltic
and Bavaria as more important objectives than Berlin. Moreover even
to plan an immediate drive on Berlin 'would be foolish in view of the
relative situation of the Russians and ourselves. . . . While it is true we
have seized a small bridgehead over the Elbe, it must be remembered
that only our spearheads are up to that river; our centre of gravity is
well back.' This smacks loudly of the sin of which all soldiers are
guilty – making the plan first and justifying it afterwards. The whole
thing, of course, was simply a question of priorities. What was the key
objective, the first priority, at this time?

The *Official History* makes the point that always predominant in
Eisenhower's mind was the military aim he had been charged with –
destruction of the enemy's armed forces and that his singleminded
determination to carry out this task was what made him believe that
going for the mythical Redoubt in the south and the naval objectives in
the Baltic would be more likely to achieve this destruction than anything else. The truth was of course that the destruction of Germany's
armed forces as far as the Western Allies were concerned had virtually
been realized and that what was now required was the *coup de grace*
actually to bring their now half-hearted and ill-coordinated defensive
efforts to an end. And as we have noted there was in this sense but one
objective – the Führer himself in Berlin. But Eisenhower did not see it
in this light. His directive issued on 18 April contained no reference to
Berlin.

Stalin's simultaneous message to the American Ambassador on the
other hand did. There was no doubt about it, 15 April was a busy day
and as Goebbels himself, although with a very different meaning, had
claimed, the second half of April was the turning point. This message
explained that the Red Army was about to renew the offensive – with
the main thrust on Dresden and a subsidiary one on Berlin. Three
fronts were to be employed – Rokossovsky's 2nd Belorussian directed
on Stettin, Zhukov's 1st Belorussian on Berlin and Konev's 1st Ukrainian moving with its right flank on Berlin while he also aimed further
west to Torgau and Dresden.

What had the Wehrmacht to withstand the forthcoming Russian

steamroller of these three army groups? General Heinrici had been in command of Army Group Vistula since 20 March. His Army Group consisted of two armies – Busse's 9th Army – which stood directly in the path between the Red Army and Berlin, and von Manteuffel's 3rd Panzer Army which stretched from north of Stettin to the Oder some 30 miles north-east of Berlin. Heinrici's first task was to eliminate the Russian bridgehead at Küstrin, and it was the events arising from the futility and failure of this operation which led to the dismissal of the one man who might even at this late stage have been able to save something from the wreck – Guderian. As soon as Heinrici in discussing the matter with Guderian in his OKH headquarters at Zossen saw what he was required to do, he proclaimed it to be quite impossible, as the attack designed by Hitler would be easily detected and the troops would then be hammered by Soviet artillery and air power. 'Our troops', he told Guderian, 'will be pinned with their backs to the Oder. It will be a disaster.' Guderian's response was uncharacteristic – a violent outburst to the effect that he had to leave then and there for another conference with the Führer who simply talked nonsense. He could get no work done. 'I spend all my time either on the road or in Berlin listening to drivel.' On the day after Heinrici's appointment and during one of his visits to Führer Headquarters, Guderian tried to persuade Himmler, as he had previously and in vain tried to persuade Ribbentrop, to go to Hitler and say bluntly that as the war was irrevocably lost and as Himmler had contacts in neutral countries, they must somehow between them arrange an armistice. Himmler objected that it was still too early for that. 'I don't understand you,' replied Guderian, 'It is not now five minutes to twelve, but five minutes past. If we don't negotiate now we shall never be able to do so.' But Himmler did nothing. That evening Hitler tried to relieve Guderian of his post, but the latter pointed out that with Wenck still unfit, and Krebs wounded, it could not be done. His dismissal was not long delayed. When on 28 March Hitler blamed Busse for the failure of the Küstrin attack and Guderian stood up for him, Hitler sent him on six weeks' convalescent leave. Krebs, who had recovered, took over as Chief of the General Staff.

Meanwhile Heinrici was wrestling with the problem of how to defend the Oder position. During his previous command of an Army on the Eastern front Heinrici had developed a technique of obliging the Russians to do an 'airshot'. It was a favourite German tactic – that of withdrawing from a defensive position under cover of darkness at the very moment when an overwhelming attack on it was imminent, so that all the weight of enemy fire power fell on nothing, and they, the enemy, suddenly came up against new, unexpected defences further on which threw them off balance and robbed their offensive of its momentum. 'It was like hitting a bag,' Heinrici himself observed. 'The Russian attack would lose its speed because my men, unharmed, would be ready. Then my troops on sectors that had not been attacked would close in and reoccupy the original front lines.' In keeping with this idea Heinrici created two general defensive positions on the Oder, so that at the right moment he could withdraw to the second, more westerly, line. Obviously his most important decision was *when* to do so. His appreciation was that the Russian attacks would not begin before mid April, and he was right. On the evening of 15 April he ordered Busse, commanding 9th Army, to move back and occupy positions in the second defensive line. It was none too soon. The withdrawal took all night. At dawn Zhukov attacked.

Also on 15 April, Albert Speer, who had long been convinced that the war was lost and who was now concerned more than anything else with saving what could be saved of the nation's industrial and communication resources, visited Heinrici at his headquarters near Prenzlau. His visit was prompted by what he had learnt of the activities of General Reymann – appointed by Hitler to be Commandant of Berlin for the approaching battle. Reymann in accordance with Hitler's nihilistic ideas had prepared all the bridges in and leading to Berlin for demolition and it was this step that Speer was determined to prevent. He had brought with him two road experts, Langer and Beck. At the subsequent conference these two technicians showed that to destroy the Berlin bridges would be to doom the city. Reymann argued that he could only defend Berlin properly if he were free to resort to every means of fighting including the destruction of bridges, and it became plain to Heinrici and Speer that he meant not only those bridges in the path of the main Russian advance, but *all* bridges – on the city's flanks and in the centre. Speer countered by pointing out that if there were to be no road access to Berlin all its industrial activities would cease and without industrial output the war could not be carried on. For a man who knew that the war was almost over, it was a quixotic argument, but an effective one, as Speer recorded :

> General Reymann was in a quandary. He did not know what to do. Fortunately, General Heinrici came to the rescue with specific orders. The explosives were to be removed from the blasting charges on the vital arteries of the Berlin railroad and highway network.

I

Bridges would be blown up only in the actual course of important military actions. After our associates had left, Heinrici turned to me again and said privately: 'These instructions will assure that no bridges will be destroyed in Berlin. For there will not be any battle for Berlin. If the Russians break through to Berlin, one of our wings will pull out to the north and the other to the south. In the north, we'll base our defence line on the east-west canal system. But I'm afraid the bridges there will have to go.' I understood. 'Then Berlin will be taken quickly.' The General agreed. 'At least without much resistance.' The next morning, 16 April, I was awakened very early. Lieutenant-Colonel von Poser and I wanted to post ourselves on a height above Oderbruck near Wriezen to watch the last decisive offensive of the war, the Soviet assault on Berlin. But dense fog prevented us from seeing anything. After a few hours a forester brought us word that all the troops were retreating and that the Russians would soon be here. So we retreated also.

In fact although it took the Red Army only ten days from the start of their offensive to surround Berlin, the Oder battle was by no means a walk-over. Heinrici's Army Group Vistula – as it was still called although it had long left the Vistula behind – stretched from the Baltic to south of Frankfurt-on-the-Oder and contained three armies – von Manteuffel's 3rd Panzer Army in the north, Busse's 9th Army in the centre, east of Berlin itself, and the 4th Panzer Army further south. One of Heinrici's critical defensive positions was on the Seelow Heights to the west of the River Oder and directly in the path of the Küstrin-Berlin road, the axis chosen by Zhukov for his main thrust. It was at Seelow that part of a Luftwaffe division with very little tactical training in ground fighting, but plenty of courage and spirit, was deployed. It was here too that the leading elements of Zhukov's army group attacked. In spite of a colossal artillery barrage and of an easy initial advance, the leading Russian troops soon ran into trouble. In particular Chuikov's 8th Guards Army (later to capture the central part of Berlin) came under concentrated fire from anti-tank guns, machine guns and artillery which caused such heavy Soviet casualties that the advancing troops were stopped. In his book *The Last Hundred Days*, John Toland reconstructed the scene from the recollections of a young *Luftwaffe* soldier who had been there:

> The din of motors and clank of tracks was tremendous. The earth trembled. . . . From behind came an abrupt, heavy-throated chorus 88 mm shells screeched overhead and smashed into the first tanks

Flames shot up, parts of metal and shell fragments rained over the foxholes. At least six tanks were on fire, but others kept coming on and on. In the reddish glare they stood out with clarity and were helpless before the withering fire of big guns. Red Army infantrymen began erupting from the middle of this massive conflagration. There must have been 800, and they scrambled up the hill shouting like madmen. . . . We fired rifles and machine guns, and hundreds of Russians toppled over. The rest came on, still yelling. More fell and at last, like a great wave that has shattered its strength against a jetty, the attackers fell back.

Zhukov did not take this setback lightly and, like most generals faced with difficulties of their own making, began to shout. When Chuikov explained that artillery from the Seelow Heights, the depth of the German defences, and the difficult going had slowed down his troops who had advanced less than a mile, Zhukov saw reason. He allowed himself the luxury of bellowing his disbelief and abuse, but then took more practical steps. He ordered his air forces and tank armies forward. Chuikov's own account of the battle predictably shows how right he himself had been about everything and how wrong his superior commander, Zhukov, was:

Before dawn Marshal Zhukov arrived at my command post. By this time the Army's troops had already taken up their starting positions. The unit commanders had gone up to the front line with the Guards' standards. The soldiers took their oath on the flag to carry out their battle assignments with honour. Flares soared into the sky, and Lenin's face looked down as if alive from the scarlet banners on the soldier-liberators, as if summoning them to be resolute in the last fight with the hateful foe. Five o'clock in the morning. . . . The second hand swept round for the last time. The darkness before dawn seemed to part, to disappear in one instant. The whole valley of the Oder rocked: forty thousand guns had opened fire. Forty thousand! It was as light as day on the bridgehead. An avalanche of fire descended on the Seelow heights. The earth reared up in what seemed an unbroken wall reaching up to the sky itself. On its far side, over there, the darkness remained; here, in the east, the dawn had broken in fire. The artillery bombardment, using every gun and mortar, and reinforced by bombers and dive-bombers, lasted twenty-five minutes. In its wake, and under cover of a double moving barrage, the infantry and tanks moved forward. Hundreds of powerful searchlights lit up the ground in front of the advancing troops. . . . The searchlights did not play the part in the attack which had been expected by the author of the idea, Marshal Zhukov. Instead of a help they became an actual hindrance. On many sectors the troops came to a halt in front of streams and canals running across the Oder valley, waiting for the light of dawn to show them clearly the obstacle they had to overcome. . . .

For the first hour and a half after the start of the offensive the enemy hardly fired at all. His command and observation posts, and his firing positions, had been overwhelmed by the shelling and bombing. Only a few machine-guns, guns and self-propelled units put up any resistance, being those which were sited in stone-built houses or in separate trenches. For the first two kilometres our rifle units and tanks advanced under cover of the moving barrage successfully, though slowly. But then the machines, which had to get past the streams and canals, began to be left behind. Coordinated action between artillery, infantry and tanks was thus lost. The moving barrage, which had been carefully calculated for a certain length of time, had to be stopped, and the artillery switched over to support of the infantry and tanks by means of consecutive concentration of fire on different points. The enemy put up particularly stubborn resistance on the Haupt canal, which runs along the valley round the foot of the Seelow hills. The spring floods had made this canal impassable to our tanks and self-propelled guns. The few bridges were under fire by artillery and mortars sited beyond the Seelow hills, and the direct fire of tanks and mobile guns which had been well dug in and camouflaged. Our air force saved the day. Our bombers and fighters, and especially the dive-bombers, had control of the air over the field of battle. They prevented the enemy's planes from putting in an appearance, and successfully suppressed the enemy artillery in the rear of his defence area. This enabled the advancing ground forces to pass the Haupt canal and begin the assault on the Seelow heights. . . .

I issued an order : at 14.00 hours, after a twenty-minute artillery raid, Seelow, Friedersdorf and Dolgelin would be attacked and the Seelow heights taken. I had no doubts of the success of this attack, but at this point once again forces intervened over which I had no control. The Front Commander, who was present at my observation post, decided to speed up the process of breaking through and seizing the positions on the Seelow heights, by throwing into the battle Katukov's 1st Mechanized Army. I requested him not to do this, since our Army had sufficient forces to carry out the assignment given it, and proposed that the general plan of the offensive should not be interfered with, but carried through systematically. I considered that until the Army had scaled the Seelow heights tank formations should not be brought into the battle; they would not perform the task, would not speed up the rate of advance. But Marshal Zhukov was not fond of withdrawing orders once given. And from midday on columns of tanks from three Corps began to move along the same few roads which were already jammed full with troops of the 8th Guards Army. The tanks made the traffic situation even worse, becoming involved with columns of motor vehicles and tracked carriers, and wrecking the manoeuvre and movement of the artillery. The forward attacking units still contrived to manoeuvre to some extent, but the reserve forces of our division, corps and army were paralysed. They were obliged to leave the roads and move, or rather creep, over the sticky, treacherous ground of the valley, across streams and canals. . . .

On the front covered by the 29th and 28th Corps, advancing to the south of Seelow, the troops had come close to the Seelow heights by evening. But a simultaneous assault on the enemy's strong points by joint forces did not prove possible, the onset of darkness did not allow us to develop the advance. The assignment for the day given us by the Front had not been carried out, the Army had not taken the Seelow heights.

By 17 April, however, Zhukov had dealt with the Seelow Heights and began to move forward again but because of further German reinforcements, his advance was still slow. Its slowness caused Stalin to order Konev to direct his armoured forces on Berlin with the result that two Soviet *fronts* were now making for the city. All this proved too much for Busse's 9th Army, and by 20 April the Germans battling for the approaches to Berlin were finally overrun. Konstantin Simonov saw the remnants of one of Busse's battle groups :

Shortly before we reached the Berlin ring road we came across a dreadful spectacle. The autobahn cut through a dense forest divided by a long clearing that disappeared into the far distance. The German troops had tried to break through to the autobahn along this clearing, and at the intersection of the two, which we reached that morning, they had suffered a devastating defeat – evidently before daybreak. This was the picture we saw : in front of us lay Berlin, and to our right a forest clearing, now a chaos of jumbled tanks, cars, armoured cars, trucks, special vehicles and ambulances.

They had uprooted hundreds of trees, probably in an attempt to turn round and escape. In this black, charred confusion of steel, timber, guns, cases and papers, a bloody mass of mutilated corpses lay strewn along the clearing as far as the eye could see. . . . Then I noticed a host of wounded men lying on greatcoats and blankets or leaning against tree trunks; some of them bandaged and others covered in blood, with no one to tend to them. . . . The broad concrete ribbon of the autobahn, already cleared and open to traffic, ran straight past this grisly scene. For two hundred yards it was pitted with craters of various size, looking like so many pockmarks, and vehicles on their way to Berlin had to weave in and out between them. . . .

General Weidling who commanded 56th Panzer Corps as part of 9th Army and suffered some of the heaviest fighting – he subsequently became Berlin Commandant – put it like this : '20 April was the most difficult day for my Corps and for all German units. They had suffered terrible losses in previous battles, were extremely exhausted and unable to withstand the great onslaught of the numerically superior Russian troops.' Despite Heinrici's declaration to Speer that there would be no battle for Berlin because his two wings would simply withdraw respectively north and south of the city, once it became clear to him that Zhukov had broken through Army Group Vistula, he did try to organize the Volkssturm battalions to conduct some sort of defence to the east of the city. But Home Guard battalions without uniforms or transport or weapons or ammunition could do little to slow down the Red Army. On 20 April Soviet artillery began to shell Berlin, and next day three armies – 2nd Guards Tank, 3rd Shock and 47th – of Zhukov's *front* reached its outskirts. Simultaneously Konev was striking forward with his 3rd Guards Tank Army. Konev's and Zhukov's two *fronts* then executed two gigantic pincer movements – one encircling the German 9th Army to the southeast of Berlin and another encircling Berlin itself. At the same time Konev's and Zhukov's leading troops pushed on towards the Elbe. By 25 April the Russians had entered Stettin, surrounded Berlin and made contact with the us forces at Torgau. All that remained now was to take Berlin and finish the war. Chuikov recorded his own memories of that day :

On 25 April 1945 the last stage of the Great Patriotic War was to begin – the storming of Berlin. On the night before it began I visited the positions of our artillery : I wanted to see the results of our ranging fire, and at the same time to imprint on my own memory the first shots fired upon the den of the Fascist beast. A battery of heavy howitzers was stationed on an open grassy space beside a wood. Dark, ragged clouds were sailing across the sky. The earth seemed to doze, shivering a little from time to time from shell-fire in the distance. The gun crews had already run out the howitzers, and were awaiting the command to fire. The muzzles were trained on Berlin. Medals 'For the Defence of Stalingrad' glittered on the chests of those serving the guns. There by the gun-carriages stand the best gun-layers of the battery, Junior Sergeants Kuprian Kucherenko and Dmitri Lapshin. There, ready to fire, is the crew's No 1, Sergeant Ivan Tarasov, Cavalier of the Orders of the Red Star and of Glory. What can he be thinking of now, this man whose brother was killed by the Nazis? Of one thing only : revenge! I know – in battle he will be grim and merciless. Everything ready for firing. 'On the fortifications of Fascist Berlin – Fire!' The heavy shells flew up, cleaving the air with a whistling sound. The path had been opened. In the morning I went up to my observation post. It was in a large five-storeyed building near the Johannisthal aerodrome. From a corner room here, where there was a jagged hole in the wall, one got a view of the southern and south-eastern parts of Berlin. Roofs, roofs without end, with here and there a break in them – the work of land-mines. In the distance factory chimneys and church spires stood out. The parks and squares, in which the young leaves were already out, seemed like little outbreaks of green flame. Mist lay along the streets, mingled with dust raised by the previous night's artillery fire. In places the mist was overlaid by fat trails of black smoke, like mourning streamers. And somewhere in the centre of the city ragged yellow plumes rose skywards as bombs exploded : the heavy bombers had already started their preliminary 'working-over' of the targets for the forthcoming attack. . . . Suddenly the earth shuddered and rocked under my feet : thousands of guns announced the beginning of the storming operation.

I looked out through the hole in the wall. There were the rings of defence works built along the Teltow, Havel and Tegel canals and the railway lines which curved round the centre of the city. There every building was a fortress. And where the walls of old Berlin rose up, there was the Nazis' most powerful defence line of all. The Landwehr canal and the sharp bend of the river Spree, its high banks clad in concrete, covered all the government offices, the Imperial Chancellery, the Reichstag. . . . The artillery continued to tear into the defence positions of the Berlin garrison. From here, high up, I could see the full, incredible force of their fire. The walls of buildings were collapsing, ramparts and street barricades went flying into the air – it was a picture impossible to transmit in words. I remember thinking then 'Hitler has committed his last and greatest crime against his own people. Why is he dooming thousands upon thousands of Germans to die, putting arms in their hands and sending them out to certain death, under oath not to give in? In the name of what is he sealing the fate of all these peaceable citizens – children, women, old men?'

As early as 1943 Hitler had employed a phrase which embodied his refusal to contemplate surrender or compromise. He had told General Thomale that if necessary he would fight until five past twelve. Guderian used the same expression to Himmler on 21 March. With Berlin encircled, were the hands of the clock at last past midnight? It looked uncommonly like it. It seemed therefore that this necessity which Hitler had foreseen had now arisen. How would the greatest strategic genius of all time conduct himself now?

10

GENIUS IN THE BUNKER

Hitler had a mind ... and his mind is, to the historian, as
important a problem as the mind of Bismarck or Lenin.

HUGH TREVOR-ROPER

There are two views of history, one determinist, the other heroic. It was perhaps Tolstoy who most strikingly illustrated the former when he claimed that no matter how much they might have believed to the contrary, Charles IX only imagined that he had decreed the Night of St Bartholemew and Napoleon only fancied that he had given the orders for his armies to march into Russia, whereas in fact these events, indeed all events, were subject to influences too numerous and complex to be comprehended by the will-power of a single man. On the opposite side of the coin we have the heroic formula concocted by Carlyle who maintained that the history of the world is but the biography of great men. If we needed a twentieth-century piece of evidence to incline us to Carlyle's reading of history, then we may not need to look much further than in the direction of the Führer. Lord Tedder is among those who so inclines and has recorded that his wartime experiences greatly emphasized for him the decisive influence exercised by individuals on the kaleidoscope of events. 'Hitler', he observed, 'was not one who was prepared to allow history to follow any predetermined political or economic course. In a megalomania fired by almost hypnotic personality he set himself to determine the pattern of the history of Europe for a thousand years.'

On 6 April 1945, a few weeks before the end of the Thousand Year Reich, its creator and destroyer sent for General Wenck (now recovered from his motor accident in February) and appointed him to command the 12th Army. The various tasks that Wenck was given underlined the absolute absurdity to which Hitler's conduct of war had deteriorated. First of all, Wenck with a mere Army, and little more

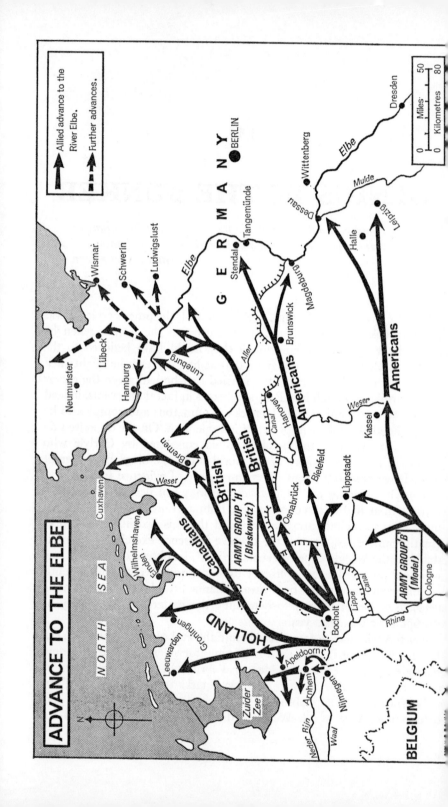

ADVANCE TO THE ELBE

Legend:
- Allied advance to the River Elbe.
- Further advances.

NORTH SEA

G E R M A N Y

BERLIN

Dresden

Wittenberg

Mulde

Elbe

Dessau

Tangemünde

Stendal

Halle

Leipzig

Wismar

Schwerin

Ludwigslust

Neumünster

Lübeck

Hamburg

Lüneburg

Brunswick

Magdeburg

Aller

Hanover

Canal

Weser

Kassel

Bielefeld

Osnabrück

Lippstadt

Bremen

Cuxhaven

Weser

Wilhelmshaven

Emden

Groningen

Leeuwarden

HOLLAND

Bocholt

Lippe

Canal

Rhine

Cologne

Apeldoorn

Arnhem

Nijmegen

Zuider Zee

Neder Rijn

Waal

BELGIUM

Canadians

British

ARMY GROUP 'H' (Blaskowitz)

Americans

Americans

ARMY GROUP B (Model)

Miles 0 50
Kilometres 0 80

than a phantom Army at that, was supposed to be able to restore the
Wehrmacht's fortunes on the Western front, a front which was being
overwhelmed by three Allied Army Groups. Then later he was to
reverse the inevitable on the Eastern front and relieve Berlin. Wenck
himself has set the record straight:

> The 12th Army was first activated at this time, in the district near
> Dessau. What were called 'Germany's last and best reserves' were
> assigned to the Army as fighting troops. Originally ten divisions were
> provided for, and the nucleus of the Army was to be comprised of
> battle-tried troops: personnel and cadets of the officer schools, excel-
> lent NCOs, experienced front officers, and many younger members of
> the Labour Service. The final orders of the 12th Army stated: Con-
> centrate north of the Harz mountains and west of the Elbe; attack
> towards the west to relieve Army Group B (Generalfeldmarschal
> Model) encircled in the Ruhr basin; and close the broken Western
> Front.

In other words he was to do what von Rundstedt and Model with far
larger forces had already failed to do – stop the Western Allies from
advancing. Small wonder that Wenck quickly realized the total inade-
quacy of his troops for the task. They were inadequate in almost every
way – in preparation, cohesion, training, concentration and numbers.
Not all their spirit, leadership or fanaticism could make up the sum
needed to stabilize an ever-changing, ever-worsening situation, a situation always subject to numerous pressures beyond Wenck's control.
With such means as this he could no more carry out his orders than call
back yesterday or bid time return. To have had any effect at all,
Wenck would have had to start committing his strength piecemeal, to
have tried to slow down the American advance before mounting a
proper counter-attack. And in any case his supposed number of
divisions simply did not materialize. He had not a single tank to his
name, nor any self-propelled assault guns, nor even any anti-aircraft
artillery at a time when the Luftwaffe's utter failure to have any
influence on what happened in the air had finally become plain for all
to see. The whole thing was a non-starter.

Nonetheless it started, but Wenck did not go far. If we exclude a
pocket in the Halle-Leipzig area, his Army never got west of the Mulde-
Elbe line at all. American pressure saw to that. Also Allied encirclement of the Ruhr was so complete that there could be no question of
his even attempting to relieve Model's forces. All Wenck could do was
to intercept and slow down some of the advancing American troops

having first concentrated his divisions in the general area Zerbst-Dessau-Bitterfeld-Wittenberg-Belzig. By mid-April something else became plain to Wenck, something so significant that it obliged him to think again about how to employ his forces. It was that the Americans were obviously consolidating on the Elbe and seemed to have no intention of pushing further east. This discovery together with the start of the Red Army's attack across the Oder made up his mind. He would use 12th Army to assist on the Eastern front. Had he been in need of confirmation and support, it was not long in coming. On 23 April Field Marshal Keitel arrived at Wenck's headquarters in Wiesenburgerforst, an unusual appearance for Keitel, Chief of OKW, rarely left Hitler's side.

Having appeared, however, he gave Wenck his orders, which were nothing if not dramatic: 'Free Berlin. Turn and advance with all available strength. Link up with the 9th Army.* Rescue the Führer. His fate is Germany's fate. You, Wenck, have it in your power to save Germany.' Stirring stuff and soon to be further reinforced by the Führer's own order of the same date, 23 April:

> Soldiers of Army Wenck! An order of great importance has called you from your concentration areas of the Western front to turn in the direction of the East. Your duty is clear: Berlin remains German. The goals ordered for you must, under all circumstances, be achieved. On other sides, operations are in progress, with the goal of dealing the Bolsheviks a decisive defeat in the battle for the German capital and thus fundamentally to alter the situation of Germany. Berlin will never capitulate before Bolshevism. The defenders of the Reich capital have taken fresh heart with the news of your fast approach, and fight with obstinacy and doggedness in the belief that soon the thunder of your guns will be heard. The Führer has called you. You have, as in old times, started on the road to victory. Berlin waits for you. Berlin yearns for you here, with warm hearts.

However warm the hearts and fervent the yearning, the road to victory had long been a *cul-de-sac* into which the Allies were herding the Wehrmacht. Wenck's understandable reaction was to burn such worthless trash. But still he carried out what he conceived to be his duty. Before we see what it was and what Wenck actually did, we must, in order to comprehend the orders at all or Keitel's appearing at Wiesenburgerforst, go back to the source of this fantastic rubbish – Berlin itself and the Bunker.

*9th Army, commanded by Busse, was deployed south-east of Berlin.

The 20 April 1945 was Hitler's 56th birthday and thus there was cause for celebration in the Bunker. The picture which Hitler presented to those who came for his birthday party was that of a man in the last stages of bodily and mental decay. While the will-power which had exercised so great and permanent an influence on those about him could still be summoned up, while the dull grey-blue eyes which often now were glazed over with a film of sheer exhaustion still seemed able to hypnotize, fascinate and compel, the actual physical state of the man was more an object of pity than of fear. Guderian's Adjutant, Captain Boldt, reported the Führer's shuffling steps, weak handshake, wobbling head, trembling hands and slack left arm – all the movements and appearance of a man prematurely senile. Yet his hesitancy and lack of decision while confirming the completeness of his disintegration were still at odds with the 'indescribable, flickering glow in his eyes, creating a fearsome and wholly unnatural effect'. Here then was genius in the Bunker. At one moment he would talk of the Russians' suffering their bloodiest defeat of the war before Berlin and at another would order all his forces astride the Elbe between Dresden and Dessau to withdraw eastwards so that the inevitable clash between the Western Allies and the Russians could be expedited. Thus the Führer oscillated between hope and indifference, utter incapacity and furious activity. Amidst all the doubts one thing was certain. On this his last birthday he and he alone was still Führer, no matter how little of the nation was left for him to lead. Führer he was to remain in name and deed until the very end.

Apart from this debatably joyous occasion, causes for celebration would not have been easy to find. Everywhere the Reich's final defences were collapsing, everywhere its enemies were assembling for the last act. Professor Trevor-Roper in his incomparable survey of Hitler's last days has reminded us of the irremediable military situation. 'Germany was now almost cut in two; only a narrow corridor of land divided the Americans, already over the Elbe, from the Russians, already over the Oder and Neisse and threatening both Dresden and Berlin. In the north, the British were in the outskirts of Bremen and Hamburg; in the south, the French were on the Upper Danube, the Russians in Vienna. In Italy, the armies of Field Marshal Alexander had captured Bologna and were pouring into the valley of the Po. And in the heart of the Reich, General Patton was thrusting through Bavaria, the cradle of the Nazi movement, towards the Alps, its intended grave.' Despite this sombre prospect, visitors to the Bunker

came to congratulate, to be received, addressed, decorated,* shaken by
the hand and dismissed.

Among the Nazi hierarchy present were Himmler,† Goebbels,
Göring, Bormann, Ribbentrop and Speer‡; among the military men
were Dönitz, Krebs¶ and of course the 'office boys' Keitel and Jodl.
To all of them Hitler was affable and confident. In the battle for
Berlin, he predicted, the Red Army would suffer its greatest defeat of
the war. But when the receptions and speeches, the congratulations and
formalities were over, it was necessary at the customary military conference to face a few facts, to face the unpalatable truth that a crisis
was at hand, that Berlin could not long survive. These disagreeable
considerations called also for some decisions to be made.

The principal topic for discussion was not so much what to do about
the well nigh hopeless military situation as what to do with the Führer
himself. If he did not leave Berlin soon he might not be able to leave it
at all, at least not by land. The main agents of the Reich's government,
such as they were – various bits of bureaucratic and administrative
machinery plus some of military direction, less the Führer's own headquarters – had already gone south to Obersalzberg. The Reich itself
was almost cut in two. It could only be a matter of time, and not much
of that, before either Berlin was finally encircled, or the enemies'
armies met, or both. To go or not to go – that was the question. At this
point Hitler was as indecisive as Hamlet. He had however to be ready,
had indeed already prepared, for the contingency of exercising command when communications with north or south were cut. His directive on the point typified both his determination to hang on to personal
control of military operations even after these operations could no
longer affect the overall strategic situation and his delusion as to controlling events by his own will-power. This directive laid down that in
an area where he was not present, a Commander-in-Chief appointed
by him would take charge of military operations and command all

*Hitler decorated members of the Hitler Youth in the Chancellory garden.

†Himmler had handed over command of Army Group Vistula to General
Heinrici on 10 March.

‡Speer, who called the Bunker the Isle of the Departed because those in it
had sealed their separation from the outer world, remembered that when heavy
bombs exploded nearby and the Bunker in spite of all the concrete and earth
on top would shake, Hitler would give a start. 'What had become of the formerly
fearless Corporal of the First World War? He was now a wreck, a bundle of
nerves who could no longer conceal his reactions.'

¶General Hans Krebs succeeded Guderian as Chief of the General Staff on
29 March.

forces on that front. If Hitler were cut off in the south, Dönitz would command in the north. If Hitler were in the north, Kesselring (who succeeded von Rundstedt on 10 March) would take charge in the south. But still 'the unified control of operations by myself personally, as hitherto, will not be altered' and 'the activity of the Commander-in-Chief of a separated area will be initiated only on special orders from me'. Even when in reality he had no control over military developments, Hitler clung to the illusion. The directive itself was to take effect at the very moment when it could have little or no influence on anything. It was in any case self-contradictory.

Yet this still did not resolve his own personal position. The truth was that Hitler had not made up his mind. Years before he had confided in Rauschning that until he was absolutely certain that this and this alone was the solution, he did nothing. What was he waiting for – Wenck's army or some unforeseeable event which would transform the military circumstances? Or was it all a game and had he long before decided that Berlin would be the scene for finally ringing down the curtain? All the members of his court, save one, urged him to go. On this occasion, however, Providence did not come up with an immediate tip. Among the entourage opinion as to what his eventual decision would be was divided. Some thought he would go, others were certain he would stay. For the time being they had to be content that this decision, like so many that had gone before and a few that were still to come, was locked in the impenetrable bosom of the Führer.

If Hitler was not willing to quit the sinking ship of state, there were plenty of others who were, not only for the comparatively non-warlike environment of Obersalzberg but simply to get away from Hitler, whose scorn, invective and threats were at once distressing and dangerous. It would be hard to imagine two men who at this time were more unlike in character, motive and intention than Göring and Speer. Göring, drug-addict, hedonist, art fancier, failed Luftwaffe commander, had long since abandoned any attempt to influence the course of the war or indeed influence anything at all except the indulgence of his own tastes. No doubt he was happy enough to remove himself from the accusing, cold, unforgiving and contemptuous gaze of the Führer before one of those oft-repeated threats as to hanging the entire Luftwaffe staff or shooting one or two to bring about a change was applied to himself. In any event he escaped, never to see Hitler again, although by what the latter described as a crass ultimatum to bring on once more a screaming outburst of rage. Exit Göring.

Speer was a horse of very different colour. Patriot, technocrat and intellectual, he refused to close his eyes to the past, the present or the future, and by his persistent examination of them was unflagging in his attempts to persuade the Führer – and when that failed persuade others – as to what was to be done to preserve at least some threads of the fabric for the German people's survival when the war, long lost in his often reiterated view, was at last over. 'When Speer came to Berlin on 20 April,' wrote Professor Trevor-Roper, 'it was not solely to congratulate Hitler on his birthday. It was to argue his cause, the sole cause that now preoccupied him, the cause of saving not the German Government, or the German Army, or the Nazi Party, but the material inheritance of the German people.' Speer had made a proper plan to realize his aims. He had prepared a broadcast to be delivered at the appropriate time which while admitting that the war was lost would also instruct the nation to hand over to the Allies all installations of any sort, industrial, military or human. He had, as we have seen, even made a pact with military commanders fighting east of Berlin that rather than contest the city and so bring about more destruction, they would withdraw westwards to the north and south of the capital. Surprisingly enough the generals had agreed. Now that he was in Berlin Speer further developed his plans and persuaded Goebbels that to destroy all the bridges leading to the city would merely paralyse its future supply no matter what else happened. Goebbels accepted that the fight for Berlin should be, so to speak, outside its walls not within them. Even Hitler himself, to whom this plan was made known, endorsed it.

Just before Speer saw Hitler, Bormann explained to him that Hitler would certainly raise the question of whether or not he should stay in Berlin or fly to Berchtesgaden. 'It's high time he took over command in south Germany. These are the last hours when it will be possible.... You'll persuade him to fly out, won't you?' Bormann wanted to live and knew that he could only do so through his master. Sure enough Hitler did ask Speer, who advised him to stay in Berlin. 'It seems to me better, if it must be, that you end your life here in the capital as the Führer rather than in your weekend house.' Hitler confirmed that this was his decision too. 'I shall not fight personally. There is always the chance that I would only be wounded and fall into the hands of the Russians alive. I don't want my enemies to disgrace my body.' Speer's description of one of the last scenes of all showed that right until the end Hitler hung on to the illusion of power, the idea that he was still in control of events, that there was still some purpose in

The Reichstag

Zhukov, Montgomery, Rokossovsky

Russian and British troops link up at Wismar, 3 May 1945

Lt Robertson and Lt Sylvashko at Torgau

having military conferences and pronouncing on which action the Wehrmacht should take :

Just then General Krebs, the Army Chief of Staff, was announced. He had come to give the situation report. In that report nothing had changed. The Commander in Chief of the armed forces was receiving situation reports from the fronts as always. Only three days before the operations room in the Bunker could hardly hold the crowd of high-ranking officers, commanders of various departments of the Wehrmacht and ss, but now almost all had left. Along with Göring, Dönitz and Himmler, Keitel and Jodl, Luftwaffe Chief of Staff Koller,* all the most important officers of their staffs were now outside Berlin. Only lower-ranking liaison officers had remained. And the nature of the reports had changed. Nothing but vague scraps of news were coming from outside. Krebs could offer little more than conjecture. The map he opened out in front of Hitler covered only the area around Berlin and Potsdam. But even here the data on the state of the Soviet advance no longer corresponded with what I had observed a few hours before. The Soviet troops had long since come closer than the map indicated. To my astonishment, during the conference Hitler once again tried to make a display of optimism, although he had only just finished talking to me about his impending death and the disposition of his body. On the other hand, he had lost much of his former persuasiveness. Krebs listened to him patiently and politely. Often in the past when the situation was clearly desperate, and Hitler continued undeterred to conjure up a favourable outcome, I had thought he was the captive of obsessional ideas. Now it was evident that he spoke two languages at once. How long had he been deceiving us? Since when had he realized that the struggle was lost : since the winter at the gates of Moscow, since Stalingrad, since the Allied invasion, since the Ardennes offensive of December 1944? How much was pretence, how much calculation?

Hitler's political testament contained a good helping of both :

After a six-years' war, which in spite of all setbacks will one day go down in history as the most glorious and heroic manifestation of a people's will to live, I cannot forsake the city which is the capital of this state. Since our forces are too small to withstand any longer the enemy's attack on this place, and since our own resistance will be gradually worn down by an army of blind automata, I wish to share the fate that millions of others have accepted. . . . I have therefore

*In fact Koller left the Bunker later.

K

decided to remain in Berlin, and then choose death voluntarily at the
moment when I believe that the residence of the Führer and the
Chancellor can no longer be held. . . .

This testament still had to be dictated. How meanwhile was Hitler,
having decided to stay in Berlin, to go on conducting the battle for it?
This was a subject of much planning, much hope, much inactivity and
eventually much recrimination. On 21 April Hitler directed his last
battle. It would be as a result of its outcome that the next step would be
taken.

He gave precise instructions to General Koller, a Luftwaffe officer
who was Göring's Chief of Staff. When Göring had left the Bunker,
Koller stayed. However well he may have understood the absolute
futility of further resistance to the Red Army, Koller was not the man
to stand up to Hitler and tell him so. He was not alone in this respect.
Serious, full of scruple and fussy, much given to examining his own
conscience and wringing his own hands, he would accept the Führer's
raving tirades full of invective and threats with cowed misgiving but
without dissent. On this occasion as so often before Hitler's orders were
couched in the greatest detail. He selected precisely which troops were
to be brought back into reserve from the northern part of the city in
order to launch a counter-attack on the Russians in the southern
suburbs. He laid down exactly which ground units of the Luftwaffe
were to be employed and in what way. To detailed deployments were
added general and wild exhortations. This attack would be in every
sense an all-out and final attempt to turn the tide. Every man who
could be mustered, every gun and every tank, even the despised Luftwaffe was invited to put every aircraft available into the skies – all
would be thrown in to savage, dismay and turn out the enemy. An ss
general, Obergruppenführer Steiner, would command the operation.

The tactical plan for Steiner's attack was that it would be launched
from the Eberswalde into the gap between von Manteuffel's 3rd
Panzer Army and Busse's 9th Army, so smashing the spearhead of
Zhukov's drive on the city. But the so-called Army Group Steiner,
which figured on Hitler's situation map, was a myth. He had nothing
like the strength required to mount an attack of the sort envisaged.
Nonetheless Hitler told him on the telephone to withdraw every man
available between Berlin and the Baltic up to Stettin and Hamburg.
The absurdity of this order is best underlined by the fact that Steiner
had no means of communicating with all these troops, let alone moving
them. Yet when Steiner protested to Krebs on the telephone that he

simply did not have sufficient men and weapons, Hitler, who was listening to the conversation, broke in with an assurance that the Russians would suffer their bloodiest defeat before the gates of Berlin. Hitler's orders were accompanied by customary threats. Commanding officers who did not thrust home would not live to tell the tale. Steiner's written instructions contained a specific promise that he was liable with his life for the execution of his orders. 'The fate of the Reich capital depends on the success of your mission.' Similarly Koller was left in no doubt that his own head would guarantee both the vigilance and totality of the effort to be made.

All was in vain. All was the mere imagining of a granite will-power which was now powerless. Hitler's drive and will-power might have helped to win battles in the past. It could prevail no more. German battalions which were mere skeletons could not overthrow Russian divisions which were fully manned and equipped. The attack never came off at all, never even crossed the start line. Withdrawal of some units in the north simply enabled Russian tanks to surge through that weakened part of the line and make their way through to the centre of Berlin. If the Steiner operation had achieved anything at all it was simply to make an already desperate military situation still more hopeless. It was this therefore – a further deterioration of his position – which Hitler now had to reckon with.

It could hardly be said that he showed the coolness so necessary in generalship when confronted with an unexpected reverse. When he discovered at the military conference next day what had happened – and what had not happened – he once more lost control of himself. The final shouting match was played out. Three hours of denouncing the generals, the staff, the German people, everybody connected with running the war except himself – this was the disagreeable scene which followed. He had been deserted; the Army had let him down; all was treason, lies, deceit, cowardly incompetence; his great mission, even the Third Reich itself, had failed; nothing was left but for him to stay in Berlin and die. If this conference left his entourage exhausted, bewildered and distraught, its effect on Hitler himself was very different. The evident need to make no more decisions seemed to calm him. There might not be much of a future to face but what remained could be faced serenely. Yet at the very moment of resigning himself to failure and death, he took the unwarranted and unforgivable step of resigning too from that great position which he had so long coveted and so long enjoyed – command of the Army. He would not delegate. He had no orders for Keitel and Jodl. He simply abdicated all responsibility. From the former position of directing the entire war machine personally, absolutely and from minute to minute, he swung fully about and would have nothing more to do with it.

No reasoning or pleading could move him. However much Jodl and Keitel might try to persuade him that after looking to him for direction for so long, they could not suddenly do without him, and whatever offers of moving troops from the west to bolster up the east might be made, Hitler would not budge from his decision. He would stay in Berlin, lead its defence and at the last moment shoot himself. Everything was falling to pieces, he could do no more, what followed could be left to Göring. When someone ridiculed the idea of fighting for Göring, Hitler retorted that it was a question of negotiation, not of fighting, and that negotiation was better in hands other than his own.

Yet even though he had just pronounced his judgment that there was precious little fighting still to be done, Hitler then fell to discussing with Keitel how Wenck's 12th Army should conduct itself in order to advance to Potsdam and save Berlin. Keitel thereupon volunteered to visit Wenck and pass on these instructions. The Führer agreed and thus it was that for once Keitel forsook his master's side and actually made his way to what might be thought of as something like the front line. With him for the first part of the journey went Jodl, the other 'office boy'. To both of them Hitler's relinquishment of his responsibilities as a soldier, moreover the 'first soldier of the Reich', was inexplicable and unpardonable. Even so Keitel confided to Jodl as they drove along that all he could tell Wenck to do was that the fight for Berlin was on and that the Führer's life was at stake – therefore Wenck must throw his entire strength into the struggle. Jodl went to Krampnitz on the western suburbs of Berlin where a skeleton staff of OKW was positioned. Although at the time Jodl might have despised his chief's abandonment of a soldier's duties, at Nuremberg he was eloquent in support of Hitler's grasping at every straw which offered itself before perishing in the ruins of his devastated capital.

With the Steiner attack a virtual non-starter, what of Wenck? Wenck's attack, which he himself described as probably the last German offensive operation of the war, began early on the morning of 26 April. Although it met with some initial success and got within ten kilometres of Potsdam, there was never any question of achieving its main task, the relief of Berlin. Wenck's own account is clear and to the point (a formula more often the purpose than the accomplishment of military pens):

The soldiers of xx Korps went in to attack in the district round Belzig and Brandenburg. They were the divisions *Schill, Scharn-horst, Hutten* and *Theodor Körner* – young soldiers who knew how things really were. They needed no special encouragement or warning orders. For weeks they had seen how urgently their help was required. When they now attacked towards the north-east, they were greeted as saviours by many thousands.

In order to make any progress at all, the troops had to leave the roads, as all routes were blocked by lines of refugees. These people had already been in the hands of the Russians, had experienced horrors and had already lost nearly all hope. Now, when they again saw German soldiers, they could draw new courage.

The young divisions went forward in good spirits, such as one remembered from the first years of the war. A whole number of Soviet units was regularly overrun and taken prisoner, including an armoured workshop and various supply columns. Where resistance was offered, it was quickly broken.

By the afternoon of 26 April the spearhead of our attack had driven 18 kilometres deep into enemy territory. As expected, the enemy had not been very strong; he had concentrated his strength near Berlin. When we reached the town of Berlitz – 25 kilometres from Berlin – we freed 3,000 wounded soldiers as well as doctors and supply personnel who had been imprisoned. . . . On the next day we reached Ferch on the shore of the Schwielowsee, about ten kilometres south of Potsdam. . . . On the afternoon of 28 April the Wehrmacht report of our thrust forward was broadcast over all available transmitters as an encouragement for the Berliners. They had to see the sign of liberation in a German advance, which had already reached the neighbourhood of Potsdam. But as a result of this broadcast, the exact extent of our front was communicated to the enemy. Our Army had now to reckon with the mobilization of all enemy troops and an attempt to annihilate us on the following day with overwhelming strength. Actually next day the enemy defences were much stronger. We attacked again on 29 April, but in spite of our courageous efforts, the attack came to nothing.

No great commander, indeed no commander whether great or not (with Wellington perhaps the sole exception) is likely to compose his valedictory despatch so as to belittle his own and his troops' efforts. Nonetheless what Wenck has to say is substantially correct. While he was pressing forward in a futile attempt to save the Führer, the Führer himself, so hard did the habit of command die, and despite renunciation of all responsibility for military operations, was fighting Wenck's battles for him, shuffling buttons about on maps in the nightmare atmosphere of the Bunker, manoeuvring phantom armies, shouting imaginary orders and behaving altogether in a Napoleonic fashion at the time when the Emperor had long ceased to pay any attention to military fact and was concerned only with the business of making pictures which fitted exactly to his own conception of events, events moreover which were conditioned altogether by his own will in order that his own empire, authority and invincibility might be preserved. Professor Trevor-Roper has left us an indelible impression of genius in the Bunker at this time :

> Pacing up and down he would wave a road-map, fast decomposing with the sweat of his hands, and explain to any casual visitor the complicated operations whereby they would all be saved. . . . No one except Hitler still believed in Wenck's army, but no one disagreed with his assurances; and in a moment of time the chorus which had been chanting *lamentoso* the dirge of despair and suicide would suddenly break out *allegro vivace* with a triumphant welcome for the army of Wenck.

At his situation conferences between 25 and 27 April Hitler had further vindicated his decision to remain in Berlin on the grounds of its somehow legalizing and morally justifying his continuing to give orders and exact retribution for others' failure. In Berlin and in Berlin alone, he insisted, could he achieve a success, even though it were a moral one, to save both face and time. He remained there in order to retain 'a moral right to act against weakness'. He could not threaten others if he himself ran away from the capital of the Reich at its critical hour. 'In this city I have had the right to give orders; now I must obey the orders of Fate. Even if I could save myself, I would not do it. The captain goes down with his ship.' As he had on a previous occasion asked Göring : 'How can I call on the troops to undertake the decisive battle for Berlin if at the same moment I myself withdraw to safety?' It was the sort of question which had not troubled Antony or James II or even the great Napoleon.

Yet when Wenck's army simply did not arrive, even the Führer began to have his doubts, had begun perhaps to wonder whether his presence in Berlin could by itself prevent the city's fall. On 28 April he sent an agitated signal to Keitel :

I expect the relief of Berlin. What is Heinrici's army doing? What is happening to the Ninth Army? When will Wenck and the Ninth Army join?*

There was no answer to these hysterical questions – at least no satisfactory answer. Rumour, as always in such cases, filled the space vacated by hard fact. Was it possible that Wenck's army had been defeated, had ceased to exist as a fighting force, or was it not more likely that the explanation for failure to carry out the Supreme Commander's impossible orders was the same as it had so often been in the past – treachery? The attack had failed because its commander had wanted it to fail. This from Hitler's point of view was the best mainstay of all. The fault lay with the generals, never with himself.

Certainly it was the supposed treachery of Himmler, as Professor Trevor-Roper has made plain, which signalled the end. Since his decision to remain in Berlin Hitler 'had waited for a week before deciding how to make an end of it; now he faced that decision. During the night of 28–29 April he disposed finally of Himmler's claim to the succession; he wrote his last will and testament; and he married Eva Braun'. For our purposes here it is important to record that in his political testament Hitler appointed Dönitz as Reich President and Supreme Commander of the Armed Forces – in other words he was the Führer's successor. A postscript to this testament was Hitler's valediction to the Wehrmacht and from it we see that even on the point of his own death he could not resist reiteration of two of his old hobby-horses – Germany's need for *Lebensraum* in the east and the German General Staff's failure to live up to its great traditions:

The people and the Armed Forces have given their all in this long and hard struggle. The sacrifice has been enormous. But my trust has been misused by many people. Disloyalty and betrayal have undermined resistance throughout the war. It was therefore not granted to me to lead the people to victory. The Army General Staff cannot be compared with the General Staff in the first world war. Its achievements were far behind those of the fighting front. ... The efforts and sacrifices of the German people in this war have been so great that I cannot believe that they have been in vain. The aim must still be to win territory in the east for the German people.

*Heinrici commanded Army Group Vistula, now west of Berlin; Ninth Army or what was left of it was commanded by Busse and was about to join up with the remnants of Wenck's 12th Army south-west of Berlin.

This postscript was given by Hitler to Colonel von Below (who had served on Hitler's staff since 1937) after the conclusion of the third of three military conferences which took place on the last day but one of the Führer's life, 29 April 1945. At the first of these conferences, held as was the custom at midday, Krebs reported to Hitler the seriousness of the situation. The Russians were closing in everywhere – from the Grunewald, from Charlottenburg and Anhalter railway stations. Ammunition supplies were inadequate. No news of Wenck, no other news at all. The only decision taken was that one more attempt to get through to Wenck would be made. Like all other attempts, it made no difference. The 4 o'clock conference produced nothing new. Things were simply a little worse if that were possible.

It remained for the final conference of the day at 10 o'clock in the evening for Hitler to play again the role he had so often played before – that of the Supreme Commander overruling the advice of his military experts. Apart from the usual gang, Goebbels, Bormann, Burgdorf and Krebs with adjutants and aides, this meeting was attended by General Weidling, Commandant of the Berlin garrison, and it was he who gave the situation report. Everywhere the Russians had advanced further and would go on advancing. At the present estimate they would capture the Chancellory itself within two or three days. Troops in Berlin must therefore start to break out of the encircled city at once. A German force of Hitler Youth still held the bridgehead on the Havel at Pichelsdorf. This was therefore the way the troops should break out. Militarily Weidling's arguments were unanswerable. Yet Hitler was not without an answer. He simply ruled that formed units could not hope to break out. Therefore no such operation would be mounted. No one questioned Hitler's decision. He had pronounced against the proposed course of action and there the matter rested.

For Hitler however there was no rest yet. Perhaps there never would be. If a Room 101 were to be imagined for him, J. B. Priestley has set it down: 'As for a Hitler – imagine him raging in his bunker, giving orders to armies already disintegrated and lost, and then in despair killing himself, finishing it all, only to find himself back in the bunker, giving those insane orders once more, and again and again and again!' What action remained to him at this point had in any case little to do with military affairs, little to do with giving orders, despite Bormann's signal to Dönitz sent at about half past three on the morning of 30 April proclaiming that Hitler, still alive, was conducting the defence of

Berlin. What Hitler had to do was to say farewell, a long farewell to all his greatness, and embark upon the ship of death. At half past three in the afternoon he had done so. The Führer had fallen. Berlin had yet to fall.

II

BERLIN KAPUTT

How pitiful is their Berlin!
ZHUKOV

While genius was at work in the Bunker, a recurring cry was constantly heard. 'Where is Wenck?' Where was Wenck as Hitler went off to study a long silence? What had happened to the 12th Army? Wenck himself answers the questions. Having failed to break through to Berlin, Wenck saw on 29 April two possible uses for his army. One was to stand firm and by holding on in the general area of Beelitz provide a sanctuary to which the Berlin garrison might itself break out. On that same day, therefore, 29 April, Wenck signalled to Weidling, Berlin Commandant, proposing exactly this course of action. He received no reply, although, as we know, it was just the same proposal that Weidling had made to Hitler that evening, only to have his ideas rejected. The second possibility for Wenck was to try and link up with 9th Army under Busse which was dithering about in an area south-east of Berlin roughly between the River Oder and Beelitz. This second idea of Wenck's was not designed to renew the offensive. It was merely that with such combined strength the two Armies might fight their way to the West together, out of the closing Soviet jaws and reach the comparative hospitality of American captivity.

Despite American action which temporarily threatened this plan, thus it transpired and by 1 May the remnants of 9th Army, 30,000 in numbers but utterly spent, without heavy weapons or supplies, reached the 12th Army area through a small bottleneck between Treuenbrietzen and Beelitz. By improvizing rail transport the men of 9th Army were moved westwards to the Elbe. No offensive operations could be contemplated. 'The idea of fighting through to Berlin in union with the 9th Army was completely absurd', recorded Wenck. 'The

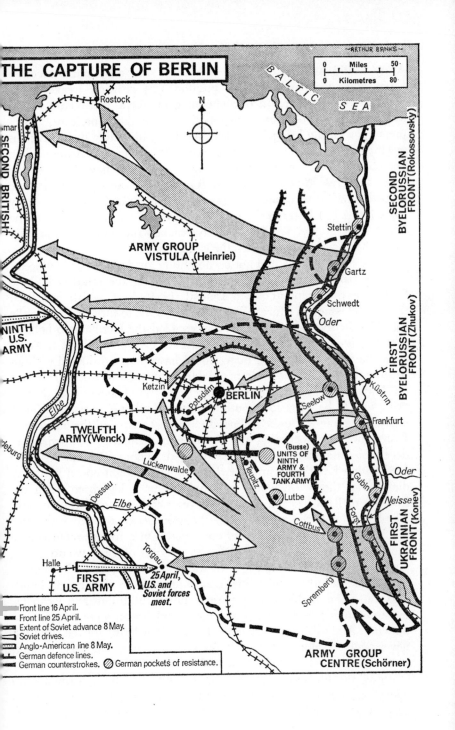

THE CAPTURE OF BERLIN

ARTHUR BANKS

| 0 | | Miles | | 50 |
| 0 | | Kilometres | | 80 |

BALTIC SEA

Rostock

N

SECOND BRITISH

ARMY GROUP VISTULA (Heinriei)

SECOND BYELORUSSIAN FRONT (Rokossovsky)

Stettin

Gartz

Schwedt

Oder

NINTH U.S. ARMY

FIRST BYELORUSSIAN FRONT (Zhukov)

Ketzin

Potsdam

BERLIN

Seelow

Küstrin

Frankfurt

TWELFTH ARMY (Wenck)

eburg

Elbe

Luckenwalde

Teupitz

(Busse) UNITS OF NINTH ARMY & FOURTH TANK ARMY

Gubin

Oder

Neisse

Dessau

Elbe

Lutbe

Forst

FIRST UKRAINIAN FRONT (Konev)

Cottbus

Halle

Torgau

25 April, U.S. and Soviet forces meet.

FIRST U.S. ARMY

Spremberg

Front line 16 April.
Front line 25 April.
Extent of Soviet advance 8 May.
Soviet drives.
Anglo-American line 8 May.
German defence lines.
German counterstrokes. ⊘ German pockets of resistance.

ARMY GROUP CENTRE (Schörner)

Army would have taken weeks to recover and gain battle strength.
From hour to hour our own position was growing weaker. The
Russians now attacked in overwhelming numbers.' Between 2 and 7
May by a series of events – negotiations with the Americans, Soviet
pressure, securing bridgeheads over the Elbe, the piling up of civilians
seeking refuge – the bulk of what was left of the two Armies, some
100,000 soldiers together with 300,000 refugees, passed across the
Elbe. General Wenck went too. 'On 7 May at 0915 hours, the
armistice according to our agreement with the United States 9th Army
came into force. Later in the afternoon, my staff and I climbed into the
last rubber dinghy. We had scarcely reached the middle of the river
when the Russians emerged on the eastern bank.'

If Busse and Wenck had not been fighting for Berlin, who had been?
Festung Berlin was, of course, a myth. Despite the renowned 'Basic
Order for the Preparations to Defend the Capital' which had been
signed and issued in March, little had been done to turn Berlin into the
sort of defensive position which had enabled the Germans to fight so
successfully and for so long in such places as Cassino or Caen. If words
could have done the trick, there would have been no difficulty about
turning the capital into an impregnable fortress, for of words there was
no shortage. Moreover the Basic Order was full of superlatives. Everything was to be done to the utmost. Every building, every shell hole,
every hedgerow was to be defended to the last man and the last round.
Every means of bettering the defences by cunning, improvization,
deception, imagination was to be employed. Every individual was to be
fired with a fanaticism, an overwhelming will to fight and if necessary
die so that the world would be required – as it had been when the
invasion of Russia began nearly four years earlier – to hold its breath.
The battle for Berlin would decide the war. Decide the war it did, but
not in the way the Basic Order envisaged. On a more practical note
there was to be an outer perimeter at a radius of some twenty miles,
another one ten miles out, a third following the S-Bahn (the railway
serving the suburbs), and a final citadel around the government buildings. But none of this made any sense unless the troops and weapons,
the ammunition and supplies and command system were adequate to
match it. And this was never to be the case. The battle for the city itself
never really developed. It was simply a gigantic mopping up operation,
at a time when the Red Army had isolated Berlin and were slowly
crushing the life out of it in overwhelming numbers. Mopping up
operation or not, except for those members of the Red Army left to
exact revenge for Leningrad or Kharkov or some other atrocities com-

mitted by the Nazis, there was little to recommend battle in a city where there were still nearly two million inhabitants and of these most were old men or children or women. It was a population which lived in its shelters. Allied bombing had seen to that and shelters which could withstand bombing could certainly withstand Russian artillery and mortars. The soldiers defending the city were still subject to some sort of disciplined organization, but that organization was a mere skeleton of what it should have been. Panzer divisions which formed part of the defending troops were equipped with a mere dozen or so tanks and armoured vehicles. When they engaged the advancing Russians, and inevitably retreated, they left the dead and wounded lying in the streets. The fighting itself was done in the midst of civilians who had themselves either been killed by rockets and shells or who were cowering in cellars, desperately trying to find further cellars behind the retreating soldiers and so not fall into Soviet hands. The streets were littered with bodies yet in some extraordinary way the spirit of the Berliners, while the war was still on, seemed to survive, and scrawled messages of defiance, proclaiming ultimate victory in spite of retreat, were everywhere to be seen. It was not the grand and glorious Götterdämmerung that Hitler had envisaged.

No properly coordinated defensive battle, of the sort that Hitler had claimed would give the Russians their bloodiest defeat, ever developed at all. There were no resources for such a course of action. Too much had been committed to the Oder and once the battle for the Oder had been lost so had the battle for Berlin itself. It was just a question of timing. Steiner's so-called attack had failed. Hitler's own conduct of the battle for Berlin, to use a phrase of his own, had been 'completely idiotic'.* Weidling on the other hand did not make the mistake of ignoring facts. On 25 April, the day on which Weidling, formerly commanding 56 Panzer Corps, became Commandant of Berlin, the city was already surrounded. That evening on making his report in the Bunker to the Führer, Goebbels, Krebs, Burgdorf, Bormann and others, he showed them from a sketch map that the ring around the city would soon be finally closed. Unknown to him the ring was closed. After explaining the dispositions of enemy divisions and German forces defending the city, Weidling went on to give his view that despite the defenders' efforts, the Russians were slowly and surely advancing to the

---

*Nearly four years earlier Hitler had angrily condemned his generals' proposals to capture Moscow – 'only completely ossified brains absorbed in the ideas of past centuries could see any worthwhile objective in taking the capital'. By the time he was defending his own capital his brain too was completely ossified.

centre of Berlin. The encircling troops were from Zhukov's 1st Belorussian *front* deployed to the east and north and from Konev's 1st Ukrainian *front* to the south and west. No fewer than eight Soviet Armies were involved. On the same day, 25 April, Hitler had signed an order laying down that the Wehrmacht's main task was to reestablish broad contact with Berlin by attacking from the north-west, south-east and south 'thus bringing the battle of Berlin to a victorious conclusion'. Like all his orders at this time – except those which could be carried out by his immediate entourage in the Bunker, such as shooting anyone who had aroused his displeasure – it was worthless. All that Weidling had, as he told Krugenberg, commanding the Nordland Division, were the remnants of his own 56 Panzer Corps, some Volkssturm (Home Guard) units, Luftwaffe ground troops and Hitler Youth, all organized into a number of defence sectors.

All these difficulties notwithstanding Weidling made a plan which he submitted to the Führer on 26 April for actually effecting Hitler's escape from the city by hacking a way through the Soviet ring. Hitler replied that he was not prepared to be caught wandering about somewhere in the woods. 'I shall stay here to die at the head of my men. But you must continue to defend the city.' In going round to inspect the defences that day Weidling saw little to reassure him. In effect Berlin was already *kaputt* :

> The Potsdamer Platz and the Leipziger Strasse were under strong artillery fire. The dust from the rubble hung in the air like a thick fog. . . . Shells burst all round us. We were covered with bits of broken stones. . . . The roads were riddled with shell craters and piles of brick rubble. Streets and squares lay deserted. Dodging Russian mortars, we made our way to the underground station by jumps. The roomy underground station was crowded with terrified civilians. It was a shattering sight. . . . He [Colonel Bärenfänger commanded in this sector] pressed me for more men and more ammunition. I could promise him neither. Most of his men were Volkssturm troopers who had been sent into the exceptionally severe fighting with captured arms. . . . No ammunition for these guns could be found in the whole of Berlin.

While Hitler was indulging in fantasies about the relief of Berlin by Wenck and while Weidling was wrestling with the actual defence of the city, the Western Allies were trying to arrive at some agreement with the Soviet Union as to an orderly arrangement for the occupation of Germany and Berlin when German resistance should be at an end.

Yet, as at Yalta, proper coordination between Great Britain and the United States was as illusory as the result of Yalta itself. Truman on becoming President was, as Roosevelt had been, bent on conciliating Stalin, and he sent Hopkins to Moscow to try and establish a better understanding between them. Neither Truman nor Hopkins was prepared to heed Churchill's warnings about Russian expansionism. Like so many American military men who had misappreciated the situation before him, Hopkins, Truman's confidant, could discern only one British motive in Churchill's anxiety to gang up with the United States against the Soviet Union – the implementation of British foreign policy in Europe. In spite of all this misunderstanding and suspicion, however, Churchill and Truman were sufficiently in harmony to send a telegram to Stalin on 27 April proposing what action was required to deal with the imminent meeting of their victorious armies :

> Our immediate task is the final defeat of the German Army. During this period the boundaries between the forces of the three Allies must be decided by commanders in the field ... it is inevitable that our Armies will in this phase find themselves in occupation of territory outside the boundaries of the ultimate occupational zones. When the fighting is finished, the next task is for the Allied Control Commission to be set up in Berlin ... and for the forces of the Allies to be redispersed and to take over their respective occupational zones. ...

Instructions would therefore be sent to Eisenhower and it was requested that the Soviet Union would similarly instruct their field commanders. No reply was received from Stalin until 2 May and then it merely stated that the respective Allied commanders would define a demarcation boundary line. But in fact Eisenhower had previously – on 22 April – suggested to the Russian General Staff that he should halt his armies on the Elbe-Mulde line on the central front, and although he offered to go further east to the Upper Elbe and push on to Dresden, a rapid Soviet answer on 24 April eagerly accepted the more westerly alignment along the rivers Elbe and Mulde. Furthermore the Russians informed Eisenhower that the Soviet Command would occupy Berlin and proposed to clean out the 'German forces from the eastern shore of the Elbe river north and south of Berlin and the Moldau river valley ...'. In other words it seemed that the Russians were proposing to take control not only of the bulk of Czechoslovakia including Prague but also of Hamburg and Schleswig Holstein. Not all Churchill's efforts prevented Prague's occupation by the Red Army, but Montgomery's quick push to Lübeck ensured that in the north the Elbe line did not, as it did in the central area, restrain the Western Allies.

John Wheeler-Bennett and Anthony Nicholls have described* the decision to halt before Prague as 'one of the most tragic errors of American military-political strategy during the post-Roosevelt era'. Yet this error was no more than history of a sort repeating itself within the space of a few weeks. On 31 March and 1 April Churchill had strongly urged on Eisenhower and Roosevelt the importance of moving on Berlin. If the Allied armies left Berlin to the Russians, he argued in a letter to the Supreme Allied Commander, at a time when the Red Army was bound to take Vienna, would not the Russians' conviction that they had done everything be so substantiated that subsequent political dealings would in consequence be all the more devious and difficult? He took an identical line with the dying President. If it should be, he pointed out, that the Russians took Vienna and Berlin, their mood would raise 'grave and formidable difficulties' from a political point of view. In short there was everything to be said politically for taking Berlin. Militarily it seemed feasible. Therefore why not do it?

How much stronger still was Churchill's later advocacy – again to Eisenhower, and this time to Truman – for taking Prague. Apart from political arguments, it would have been so much easier militarily. 'There can be little doubt,' he wired Truman at the end of April, 'that the liberation of Prague and as much as possible of the territory of Western Czechoslovakia by your forces might make the whole difference to the post-war situation in Czechoslovakia . . . of course such a move by Eisenhower must not interfere with his main operations against the Germans, but I think the highly important political consideration mentioned above should be brought to his attention.' To Eisenhower himself Churchill signalled the hope that his plan would not prevent an advance on Prague. 'I thought you did not mean to tie yourself down if you had the troops and the country was empty. . . .' Eisenhower had the troops all right and at that time the country was empty. But not for long and then not even the Czechs' own appeals could prevail. The Red Army was to win all. It occupied Prague, Vienna and Berlin.

It remained to be seen exactly how Berlin itself would fall. Lt Col Pavel Troyanovsky was a correspondent with the Red Army, and his account is representative of what happened:

At 4 o'clock on 21 April General Perevertkin took over a new

* *The Semblance of Peace*, London, 1972.

11th Hussars in Berlin, 6 July 1945

US Sherman tanks in Berlin, 4 July 1945 Potsdamer Strasse

observation post on the outskirts of the Berlin suburbs, Weissensee. 'Well, there's Berlin, feast your eyes on it!' said the General. Field glasses were now unnecessary to see the wide vista of the German capital. From one end of the horizon to the other stretched houses, gardens, factory buildings and chimneys, and many churches with their sharp spires reaching to the sky. . . . Volumes of smoke arose from all quarters and hung like a pall over the city. The German capital was burning. The thunder of the artillery bombardment shook the air, the houses and the ground. And Berlin replied with thousands of shells and bombs. . . . It seemed as though we were confronted not by a town, but by a nightmare of fire and steel. Every house appeared to have been converted into a fortress. There were no squares or gardens, but only gun positions for artillery and mine throwers. . . . Our guns sometimes fired a thousand shells on to one small square, a group of houses or even a tiny garden. Then the German firing points would be silenced, and the infantry would go into the attack. . . . From house to house and street to street, from one district to another, mowing their way through gun fire and hot steel, went our infantrymen, artillery, sappers and tanks. . . . On 25 April the German capital was completely encircled and cut off from the rest of the country. At the height of the street fighting Berlin was without water, without light, without landing fields, without radio stations. The city ceased to resemble Berlin. . . .

Whether the city was recognizable or not, Stalin's order of 23 April to Zhukov and Konev had laid down the boundary between them which would extend from Lübben (his former junction point) to Teupitz, Mittenwalde, Mariendorf, Anhalter Station. In other words the Reichstag, the main prize where the Soviet flag was to be raised, was given to Zhukov. His soldiers captured the Reichstag building and ran up the Red flag at about 2.30 on the afternoon of 30 April – an hour before Hitler committed suicide. But German resistance continued from the Reichstag cellars even after the rest of the building's capture. A German anti-aircraft NCO recorded how an SS officer conducted the defence during the last few days of the battle for Berlin :

The close combat boys went into action. Their leader was SS-Obersturmführer Babick, battle commandant of the Reichstag. I was acting as runner between the AA gunners and the SS battle group, a part of the Nordland SS Division. Its headquarters were in Europa House near the Anhalter Railway Station. Babick now waged the kind of war he had always dreamed of. Our two battery commanders, Radloff and Richter, were reduced to taking orders from him. Babick's command post was not in the Reichstag itself but in the cellar of the house on the corner of Dorotheenstrasse and the Hermann-Göring-Strasse, on the side nearer the Spree. There he ruled from an air-raid shelter measuring some 250 feet square.

Against the wall stood an old sofa and in front of it a dining-table on which a map of the centre of Berlin was spread out. Sitting on the sofa was an elderly marine commander and next to him two petty officers. There were also a few ss men and, of course, ss-Obersturmführer Babick bending over his map. He played the great general and treated everyone present in the dim candle-lit room to great pearls of military wisdom. He kept talking of final victory, cursed all cowards and traitors and left no one in any doubt that he would summarily shoot anyone who abandoned the Führer.

I had no difficulty in reaching this 'battle station' through an underground passage beneath Hermann-Göring-Strasse. As I remember, there was a thick central-heating pipe which presumably ended in the Prussian Landtag. It was my job to carry Babick's orders to my unit. The shelling of the Reichstag never stopped for a moment. During the short periods I spent in Babick's headquarters, I always heard what the latest position was. I was told yet another Russian shock detachment had tried to enter the upper storeys of the Reichstag but had been wiped out. Babick was tremendously proud of his successes. He was hoping for reinforcements. From somewhere or other, marines had come to Berlin on the night of 28 April, led by the very Lieutenant-Commander who was now hanging about the cellar with nothing to say for himself. Babick never moved from his map, plotting the areas from which he expected reinforcements and even the arrival of 'Royal Tigers' (heavy anti-tank guns mounted on Tiger tank chassis).

Babick was still bubbling over with confidence. For one thing, he thought himself perfectly safe in his shelter. ss sentries were posted outside, others barred the corridor to the Reichstag, and Royal Tigers, our finest weapons, were apparently just round the corner. He had divided his men into groups of five to ten. One group was commanded by ss-Untersturmführer Undermann (or something like that; I didn't get the name quite clearly); he was posted south of the Moltke Bridge in the Ministry of the Interior (the building the Russians called 'Himmler's House') and the bridge itself lay in his line of fire.

Then an ss ensign, aged about nineteen, came to Babick with the report that Undermann and his men had come across some alcohol and that they had got roaring drunk. As a precaution he had brought Undermann along; he was waiting outside. Babick roared out the order: 'Have him shot on the spot.' The ensign clicked his heels and ran out. Seconds later we heard a burst of fire from a sub-machine-gun. The boy reappeared and reported: 'Orders carried out.' Babick put him in charge of Undermann's unit.

Our ranks in the Reichstag got thinner and thinner. Part of our battery gradually dispersed, and by the night of April 30, no more than forty to fifty people, soldiers and civilians, were left in the cellar. This remnant was now busy looking for the safest possible hiding-places. There we intended to sit tight until the Russians came. But they kept us waiting for another twenty-four hours. At dawn on May 1, we heard over our portable radio that the Führer had 'fallen in the battle for the Reich Capital', his wife at his side. Goebbels and his family had gone the same way. We were our own masters, at long last.

Zhukov's own account of the final phase in spite of its somewhat ponderous self-adulation is worth remembering:

At 1.50 pm on 20 April the long range artillery of the 79th Rifle Corps of the 3rd Shock Army was the first to open fire against Berlin, thus laying the basis for the historic assault on the German capital. The next day elements of the 3rd Shock Army, the 2nd Guards Army and the 47th Army broke into the outskirts of Berlin and engaged the battle in the city. We also decided to throw the 1st and 2nd Guards Tank Army into the battle to end the enemy's morale and will to fight, to give maximum support to our weakened field armies and thus speed the capture of Berlin. The battle soon reached its culmination. We all wanted to finish it off by the 1 May holiday to give our people something extra to celebrate, but the enemy in his agony continued to cling to every building, every cellar, floor and roof. The Soviet forces inched forward, block by block, building by building. The troops of Generals Kuznetsov, Berzarin and Bogdanov moved closer and closer to the centre of the city. And finally I received the long awaited call from Kuznetsov: the Reichstag had been taken; our red banner had been planted on it and was waving from the building. What a stream of thoughts raced through my mind at that joyous moment! I relived the crucial battle for Moscow where our troops stood fast unto death, envisioned Stalingrad in ruins but unconquered, the glorious city of Leningrad hold-

ing out through its long blockade of hunger, the thousands of
devastated villages and towns, the sacrifices of millions of Soviet
people who had survived all three years, the celebrations of the
victory of the Kursk salient – and now, finally, the goal for which
our nation had endured its great sufferings; the complete crushing of
Nazi Germany, the smashing of Fascism, the triumph of our just
cause.

The great question now was how to negotiate with the Russians and
how to surrender the city or what was left of it, for by this time only the
Government buildings, part of the adjoining Tiergarten and the area
between the Zoo and the Havel river remained in German hands.
Hitler had specifically forbidden Weidling to capitulate, but he had
authorized a break-out. Meanwhile Bormann and Goebbels took a
hand in affairs. Bormann had sent a telegram to Admiral Dönitz in
Plön immediately after Hitler's death, appointing him to be Hitler's
successor. Dönitz, not realizing that Hitler was dead, replied: 'My
Führer! My loyalty to you will be unconditional. I shall do everything
possible to relieve you in Berlin. If Fate nevertheless compels me to rule
the Reich as your appointed successor, I shall continue this war to an
end, worthy of the unique, heroic struggle of the German people.' But
at the same time Goebbels and Bormann were trying to bring the
struggle to an end without more ado. Contact was made with the
Russian headquarters and they agreed to receive a representative of the
German Government.

The Chief of the General Staff, Krebs, who spoke Russian and had
served in Moscow as Military Attache, was chosen as the German
emissary. His talk was with Chuikov, Commander of 8th Guards Tank
Army, at Schulenburgring near Tempelhof airport. Krebs arrived
there at about 4 am on the morning of 1 May. He had been authorized
to negotiate only a truce or armistice so that surrender arrangements
between the new German Government and the Russians could then
begin. Despite Russian suspicions that the Western Allies were at this
time contemplating a separate peace with the German armies in the
West, Chuikov and his advisers refused to consider anything short of
unconditional surrender. When Krebs tried to introduce a more genial
note into the discussions by referring to the First of May as a day when
their two nations shared celebrations and enjoyed a great holiday,
Chuikov countered by observing that while it might be a fine day in
Moscow, he could not say whether it were the same in Berlin. So
Krebs' attempt failed and he himself committed suicide after returning

to the Bunker. Next it was to be Weidling's turn to try his hand at negotiation. On the following morning he crossed the line dividing the two armies and surrendered the Berlin garrison with its 70,000 troops. The battle for Berlin was over.

Indeed the war itself was almost over. Everywhere the story was one of capitulation by the Germans and a race for position by the Allies. Some days earlier, on 29 April, General Wolff, head of the ss in Italy and acting for von Vietinghoff, Commander-in-Chief South West, had signed an armistice. Fighting in Italy ended on 2 May. In Stockholm on 30 April a German emissary had reported that Busch, Commander-in-Chief North West, would capitulate as soon as the British got to the Baltic and made sure of Schleswig Holstein and Denmark. Next day they had done so. Montgomery's forces had driven across the Elbe on 29 April reaching Lübeck and Wismar on 1 May and so beating the Russians to it by a single day.

Before this, British troops fighting their way into Bremen reenacted the capture of Berlin on a tiny scale. A member of the 4th Royal Tank Regiment recalled their last battle :

The attack went in on 27 April. In one sector of the city only did the Germans really resist. This was in the park to the north when the garrison commander, surrounded by a pack of fanatical ss men went to ground in the air-raid shelters, and from there tried, without success, to harry the flanks of our advance. Each troop of tanks with its affiliated infantry had its own little objective to capture. As the attack moved deliberately forward, the opposition was from snipers and every now and then a salvo of shells crumping down from the German guns to the north. Our own guns kept up a steady and heavy fire on the air-raid shelters of the ss men and succeeded in keeping them to ground. At first there were few civilians to be seen, but soon, with growing confidence, they started to fill the streets. Their relief that no battle was to be fought over their heads was such that soon we were being hailed as liberators. As the tanks reached the centre of the city, hundreds of slave workers rushed forward. Each appeared to have a bottle and in no time the most riotous scenes were in progress. . . . Now we were getting into the really flattened sectors of the city. Huge bomb craters and massed rubble blocked the roads while the tram wires, straggling at all angles across the street were a formidable obstacle too. Many a tank commander going forward with his head out of cupola was nearly decapitated. It took a long search to find our way through, but by the evening all objectives were in our hands and the infantry engaged in detailed searching of buildings, factories and workshops. That night we leaguered amongst the infantry in the city but there was little sleep. The whole night long, drunken celebrations of our arrival was continued by the liberated slaves.

Many more slaves were soon to be liberated when on 3 May Dönitz sent a delegation under Admiral von Friedenburg to Montgomery at Lüneburg to negotiate surrender. By the evening of the next day all German forces on Montgomery's front – that is in North-West Germany, Denmark, Holland and, ironically enough, Dunkirk – had surrendered. The agreement was to take effect from 8 am on the following morning, 5 May. Von Friedenburg then went on to Eisenhower's headquarters at Rheims, where he was told that the German High Command must surrender without conditions and simultaneously on the Western and Eastern fronts. Dönitz accepted this and at 2.41 on 7 May Jodl signed the instrument of surrender to take effect at midnight on 8 May. Having done so Jodl made a point to remember: 'With this signature the German people and the German armed forces are for better or worse delivered into the victors' hands. . . . In this hour I can only express the hope that the victors will treat them with generosity.' Had the Germans been dealing with Churchill alone this hope might have been realized. But not all the victors believed as he did in magnanimity.

A further formal surrender was signed by Keitel and Zhukov in Berlin on the night of 8–9 May. As far as the wartime Allies were concerned, it was marred by disagreements, which were petty in relation to the conflict being brought to an end. Vishinsky, Zhukov's political adviser, would not at first agree that Spaatz and de Lattre de Tassigny could sign on behalf of their countries in addition to Zhukov and Tedder. Hours of wrangling followed further disturbed by bad seating arrangements, an arrogant attitude by Keitel and some muddle over what pens were to be used for signing. If not a glorious end to Allied wartime collaboration, it was at least a fitting prelude to Allied peacetime rivalry. And one of the most spectacular and dangerous manifestations of this rivalry was to concern control of Berlin. The Russians, of course, were already in occupation of the city. The British and Americans had still to arrive. Russian soldiers predictably behaved like barbarians, like the *Untermenschen* that the Nazis had always said they were. One woman recalled it like this:

Strange how the first thing they ask is invariably: 'Have you a husband?' If one says No, they promptly begin to slobber at the mouth. If one says Yes, hoping to be left in peace, then the questioning continues: 'Where is he? Was he taken at Stalingrad?' If, on the other hand, one has a living husband whom one can produce (as the widow does with Herr Pauli, although he is nothing but her lodger) then they first of all step back a pace. Not that it matters to them whom they get, for they have no compunction about taking married women, but they prefer not to have husbands hanging around, so they invent devices to get them out of the way, have them locked up or sent off. Not, by any means, from fear, for they have already found out that no husband here is likely to cause them much trouble. So long as they are not completely drunk, however, a husband on the premises does disturb them.... A woman in the water queue told me how a man in her cellar had shouted at her when Ivans were trying to drag her away: 'Go along, for God's sake! You're getting us all into trouble!'

Rape, looting, burning and murder were common. Hitler's very last War Directive of 15 April had made it clear what fate threatened a defeated Germany. 'While the old men and children will be murdered, the women and girls will be reduced to barrack-room whores.' Even at the end Hitler's reliance on propaganda and foresight did not desert him. But better things were on the way for Berlin. The Red Army positioned more disciplined regiments there; American troops reached the city on 1 July; the British arrived next day. Richard Brett-Smith remembered his own entry on 4 July:

Just after four o'clock the column drew to a standstill on the Pichelsdorferstrasse, some half a mile away from the saluting base.... Everyone is tired and dusty, but in good heart. We decide there is time (as there always is for the British soldier) for a quick cup of tea, and after that we are off again.... Berlin has been for so long the hub around which so many hopes and fears and jokes and allusions revolved, that only by reaching the city can we really seem to have won the war ... the dark crowd of Germans lines the pavements and clusters in knots on the uneven rubble ... they gaze fixedly, but many smile and some wave, a few almost cheer. It is indeed more like a sober liberation welcome than a triumphant entry into a conquered city, and for that without doubt, we have the Russians to thank. Who could ever have foretold that when we entered Berlin we would come as liberators, not as tyrants, for the Germans? ... At last, then, we come to von Seeckt barracks in Spandau.... Dusk

falls ... all-healing night covers the torn and shattered city. . . .
Sleep on, Berlin, for you have many cares.

Not the least of these cares was the establishment of inter-Allied control
of the city. Although as early as 5 June Zhukov and Eisenhower agreed
on the three great proclamations which respectively gave supreme
authority to the Allied Commanders-in-Chief, stipulated that only
unanimous agreement between them could constitute authority for
matters affecting Germany as a whole, and fixed the boundaries of the
four Berlin zones, it was not until 30 July that the Allied Control
Council held its first meeting. Before that the military men had on the
whole got on quite well together. Indeed Zhukov observed to General
Weeks on one occasion that they could achieve a great deal as long as
the politicians would keep out. Unfortunately the politicians did not
keep out – they never will keep out – and Berlin became a limb need-
ing constant attention and nourishment. But at least the limb did not
wither nor did it have to be amputated.

Jodl's hope that the victors would treat the vanquished Germans
with generosity might have been applied also to the victors' treatment
of one another. Decision making on the battlefield might be over for
the time being, but decision making at the conference table was not.
One more such conference, or rather part of one, with his victorious
Allies was to be granted to the great Churchill. During it he handed
over the Premiership. He made no subsequent secret of his disappoint-
ment and dismay with what happened at Potsdam in July 1945. He
even went so far as to argue that had he remained in power it would
not have happened:

> The line of the Oder and the Eastern Neisse had already been
> recognized as the Polish compensation for retiring to the Curzon
> Line, but the overrunning by the Russian armies of the territory up
> to and even beyond the Western Neisse was never and never would
> have been agreed to by any Government of which I was the
> head. . . .
>   The real time to deal with these issues was . . . when the fronts of
> the mighty Allies faced each other in the field, and before the
> Americans, and to a lesser extent the British, made their vast retire-
> ment on a 400-mile front to a depth in some places of 120 miles, thus
> giving the heart and a great mass of Germany over to the
> Russians. . . .

The heart – what if Churchill had had his way earlier and the Western
armies had met the Russians not on the line of the Elbe-Mulde rivers,

but on the Oder-Neisse line, with Berlin in their own hands? What then? How different a Potsdam conference might have been. Even the administrative arrangements would have been made by us. Churchill's fundamental dislike of allowing the Russians to occupy great chunks of Central Europe was that he could see no future for these areas unless it was acceptable to, that is controlled by, the Soviet Government. And that to him was no future at all. Yet all this apart, the American view – and we are speaking of a time when in Western counsels the American view usually prevailed – was that the Western Allies were committed to a definite line of occupation and that this commitment must be honoured. Churchill, too, was in favour of honouring commitments provided all of them were equally honoured, in other words provided the Western Allies could be satisfied that the entire European future was being properly settled. At Potsdam American support for such a notion was not to hand. 'Even at Potsdam the matter might perhaps have been recovered, but the destruction of the British National Government and my removal from the scene at a time when I still had much influence and power rendered it impossible for satisfactory solutions to be reached.' Whether Churchill would have succeeded may be questioned, but there is no question but that he would have tried.

Yet the reasons for what followed, and what is usually known as the Cold War, have not always been properly understood. A reviewer of *The Semblance of Peace*, already referred to, makes the real reasons much plainer. He points out that its genesis was in events much earlier than 1945. 'The emergence of Truman and Attlee, Byrnes and Marshall and Bevin, crystallized an antagonism which they did not create.' All the elements of the Cold War were there when Stalin, Churchill and Roosevelt were calling the odds. They called them with such uncommon skill that stability of a sort was maintained. It was not divergent policies which changed after 1945, but the men and measures which gave voice to these policies. Above all it was the attitude of Stalin. 'Before Potsdam he knew that he was confronted by British and American leaders who were deeply divided among themselves and of whom the American were basically anti-British. . . . After Potsdam he found that the Anglo-American differences were no longer going to be played out before his eyes, even if they still existed . . . the aims of Western policy had not changed : they had only been sharpened and stiffened. The Cold War was Stalin's reaction.'*

If any single city symbolized the Cold War, that city is Berlin.

* *Times Literary Supplement,* 22 September 1972.

WHOEVER CONTROLS BERLIN . . .

Berlin will remain the sore thumb of Western Europe.

PHILIP C. JESSUP, 1971

The word unique is not simply overworn; it is constantly misused. Applied to the city of Berlin however it is superlatively apt. What other city, which since the eighteenth century has been the capital of a powerful European nation, is divided and occupied by foreign troops whose commanders wield ultimate authority in its administration? What other city has a hideous concrete wall with mined deathstrips across and around it? What other city has been a pawn in the international game of chess for so long and with such dangerous potentialities? What other city has both been destroyed and saved by air power? What other city, even today, faces so uncertain a future and is the cause of quite so many negotiations – negotiations designed by irreconcilable parties to resolve once and for all this enduring uncertainty? About Berlin's uniqueness we need not be in doubt.

This uniqueness began with its handover to quadripartite control. All the unconditional surrenders which took place in May 1945 and which we glanced at in the last chapter were military. Now at last – and we are speaking of a time when there was no central political authority for Germany with whom the Allies could deal – the moment came for establishing 4 power control of Germany in Berlin. This in turn meant the division of the city itself into four. But it was not until 4 June 1945 that the European Advisory Commission had been able to reach the point when they could advise the four governments concerned that their Commanders-in-Chief should meet in Berlin to sign a Declaration of Defeat and Assumption of Supreme Authority and thus legally clear the way for establishing the Control Commission and the Kommandatura. If the Kommandatura itself is long since extinct, at

least the building housing it has survived and is used still for negotiation among all four powers of which it was originally composed. What
has all the negotiation been about? It has been at times both protracted
and fruitless. It has led to dangerous confrontations. Striving to better,
oft we mar what's well. What *is* well is that negotiations continue.

What is the reason? Is it to be found in Lenin's well-known declaration that whoever controls Berlin will rule Germany and whoever
controls Germany rules Europe? Indeed would Lenin's point, coined at
a time when Imperial Germany had once again demonstrated to the
world that the central problem of Europe was still the German question, have any meaning today? Who does control Berlin? Control is –
and it is a most fortunate circumstance – multilateral. The Berliners
themselves, east and west, the Soviet Union, the German Democratic
Republic, the Federal Republic of Germany, France, Great Britain
and the United States – these eight between them say what is to
happen in Berlin. No doubt there are other influences. Other countries
of the Warsaw Pact and NATO and indeed any nation with whom the
eight principal controllers have relations of one sort or another make
their mark. But in essence the eight call the tune, and a very jangled
tune it is. Do these eight also rule Germany? It would be hard to refute
it. The so-called Four Powers, wartime allies and peacetime competi-
tors, still have special rights and responsibilities not only for Berlin in
particular but for Germany as a whole. These are not mere words.
However futile the idea might be that 4 power harmony in running
German affairs could ever be restored, the three Western countries,
France, Britain and America, do have great influence on the domestic
and foreign policy of the *Bundesrepublik* and the Soviet Union does
still lay down the law to Herr Honecker and his men when the issues
are beyond those of mere internal trivialities.

If the two Germanies and their respective sponsors effectively have
the say as to what goes on in the Federal Republic of Germany and the
German Democratic Republic, can they as a bunch be said also to
control Europe? Not every inch of it perhaps, but there is only one set
of conductors in whose hands the baton which orchestrates Eastern
Europe remains – the clique surrounding Brezhnev. And when we
think of Western Europe, do we think of Denmark and Spain, Luxem-
bourg and Austria? We do not. We think primarily of France,
Germany and Great Britain; we think of NATO and the European
Economic Community; we remember that the United States manipu-
lates a good many of the wires both on and off stage. So that in a way
unimaginable to its author, Lenin's dictum still holds good.

Is the present state of affairs likely to endure? There are those who maintain that the signing of the Berlin Quadripartite Agreement in September 1971 introduced a new set of circumstances in which the bone of contention, which the city itself represented, would finally be put aside. It may be that not all of us would agree with this. Our judgment would do well to run parallel with the facts. On the one hand the signing of the Berlin Agreement was a remarkable event. For here after all we had the Soviet Union actually sitting down with the three Western Powers and making it clear that it was no longer her policy to turn these three Powers out of Berlin. We had the Soviet Union actually guaranteeing civil access to and from the city and recognizing that links between West Berlin and Bonn should be continued and developed. What is more the Soviet Union succeeded in persuading the GDR to acknowledge and accept all this. Here are some facts. But another fact, on the other hand, which stands out more speakingly than any is that since the GDR in subsequent dealings with the FRG became party to an agreement guaranteeing access to and from Berlin, the GDR's own claim to have some say in what happens on those access routes by air, rail and road which pass through her territory was accordingly reinforced.

Since that time there have been further and faster developments. The Four Powers' continued rights and responsibilities for Berlin and Germany have been reaffirmed. A General Relations Treaty between the two Germanies has been concluded and ratified. Herr Brandt, the great architect of *Ostpolitik*, has been returned to office with a strengthened position. Recognition of the GDR has gained irresistible pace and Western countries are falling over themselves to establish embassies in East Berlin. The Soviet Union will soon have its Consulate in West Berlin. The two Germanies themselves have exchanged diplomatic missions and have concluded arrangements for their entry into the United Nations. Yet none of these changes alters the GDR's capability to turn a railway light to red or leave in position a barrier on the autobahn.

What is Berlin's position now that the FRG and the GDR are both in the United Nations? What will be the effect on East Berlin when it is thronged with embassies from Western Europe and the rest of the world, its airport at Schoenefeld perhaps fielding more traffic than all three West Berlin airports (Tegel, Tempelhof and Gatow) put together? In such circumstances could West Berlin – never to be the capital of the FRG as East Berlin is of the GDR – begin to wither on the vine? Not, we may suppose, if the Western Allies stand firm, continue to maintain their garrisons in the city, continue to insist on their rights of access, while the Federal Republic itself continues to develop links with West Berliners, still foots the bill for the substantial subsidies without which the city's administrative expenses could hardly be met. Will the Allies stay and if so for how long?

It is too early to read the outcome of a Conference on European Security and Cooperation, but if this does no more than acknowledge the *status quo,* including that of Berlin itself, then we may perhaps draw one conclusion – that in keeping footholds in Berlin and in continuing to have a say in German affairs generally, Soviet and Allied interests converge. Long may they do so. The Berlin Agreement therefore may be said not to have changed anything, but merely formally to have recognized a state of affairs that has long prevailed. Equally unchanged, however, is the fact that Berlin is still 100 miles or so east of the still iron curtain. There has been no peace treaty. There has been no formal alteration in the political status of West Berlin, however formal the treatment of East Berlin as the GDR's capital may be, and however proscribed the Western Allies' supposed rights in this new capital may have become. Berlin remains divided. Germany remains divided, no matter how much soothing talk may be contained in the General Relations Treaty about two states within one nation.

The battle for Germany is not over, is indeed in its present phase only just beginning. It will not be fought with bullets. Jaw-jaw has mercifully taken over from war-war. Berlin remains the meeting point, where West Berliners and citizens of the FRG flow into the GDR and its capital. Cut off that source of communication and a major tactical loss would be suffered by the Western Allies. So that in a curious way, just as the fall of Berlin in 1945 heralded the end of that war against Germany, so the fall of Berlin in this or the next decade might herald the end of better understanding between Germany's two parts. As long as the German question remains central to European security, as long as Berlin remains central to the German question, so long will the battle for the city – in no matter what muted tones – rage. It must not be taken by the Russians a second time.

No one would be foolish enough to regard Russian aims as being benevolent to the West. Of course they wish to detach West Germany from NATO; of course they wish (and will encourage the GDR to do the same) to deal with Bonn more and more on a bilateral basis and not in a Four-power context; of course they see *Ostpolitik* in terms of absorbing West Germany into an arena of eastern influence. General Reinhard Gehlen (Guderian's Intelligence adviser) who spent a military lifetime studying 'Foreign Armies East' still maintains that the hinge of the Soviet Union's efforts for a 'peace' settlement will 'remain West Germany, which they will try to undermine, isolate and intimidate as a preliminary to transferring her to the Soviet sphere of influence'.

Yet no issue of this sort can be seen in such simple terms. Opening the door to allow your own influence to emerge opens it too for other influences to enter. Indeed for the first time perhaps Berlin may be used as a lever in the hands of Bonn to ensure Russian good behaviour in exchange for continued economic and technological aid. That much is plain. If the Soviet Union hopes to secure the isolation of West Germany from a policy of general détente in Europe, the Western Allies hope to dissolve the isolation of Eastern Europe by the same process. Security and Cooperation have different meanings in different countries. Compromise will no doubt have a large hand in affairs. But it is Berlin itself which still provides the vehicle for consultation, cooperation and compromise. Therefore no matter what else might happen, the Western Allies must stay in Berlin. Whoever controls Berlin. . . . Let it not be controlled by the demagogues of Moscow and Pankow. In contemplating them, together with the greatest demagogue in history whose manipulation of power in and beyond the Third Reich brought about the battle for Berlin in the first place, we might do well to remember an observation of Charles Pierre Péguy. 'The triumph of demagogues is short-lived. But the ruins are eternal'.

EPILOGUE

History is not just a catalogue of events put in the right order like a railway timetable. History is a version of events.

A. J. P. TAYLOR

We began with Macaulay and we might find it hard to do better than end with him. If ever it were necessary to lend further weight to Professor Taylor's point as to what history is, then surely Macaulay's great work provides it. It is no more than a version of events – incomparable no doubt in the mastery of its narrative, the detail of its scholarship, the power of its description and the grandeur of its style, but a version nonetheless. Its purpose was of course to proclaim the greatness of England's, that is to say the Whigs', political and material achievements. One feature of this particular version was emphasized by Sir Charles Firth who pointed out that for the sake of displaying one giant – William III – Macaulay peopled all Europe with pygmies. He is not so unwise as to suggest that William was the greatest exponent of military skill in the War of the Grand Alliance or the most regular winner of battles. He is the first to recognize the superior claims of such men as Luxemburg and Marlborough. It is William's felicitous combination of political sagacity and military competence, tempered with a large dose of common sense and further welded together by courageous determination – and his championship of the Whigs – that make William Macaulay's hero. That he needed all these qualities is well demonstrated by his able handling of the difficulties inherent in any sort of coalition. When Disraeli observed that England did not love coalitions, he was, as we know, referring to the coalition of political parties. In military coalitions on the other hand, while perhaps not loving them, England has repeatedly indulged. William found, like Marlborough and Anne, like Wellington and Pitt, that coalitions sponsored by England are usually kept together with English gold. Yet in the case of another Grand Alliance, presided over by another Churchill, it was not English gold that did the trick for by the time England had lost most of her colonies and all the Allies she began the war with, there was precious little English gold left. Churchill, who like Nelson regarded writing about great deeds as second best only to performing them, produced *his* version of events, and as might have been supposed bestrides his particular world like a Colossus.

Yet if we read almost any other book about the Second World War which either deals with the European part of it or with the conflict in general, it is not Churchill who is the dominant figure. There is but one giant who is, so to speak, on stage all the time, and that giant is Hitler. All the rest, Churchill, Roosevelt, Stalin, de Gaulle, if not pygmies, are by comparison the supporting cast. For it was Hitler who more than any other single military or political leader called the strategic tune, certainly for four of the war's six years, and even later at the time when his title hung loose about him like a giant's robe upon a dwarfish thief. Allusions to Macbeth stick closer when we read in an introduction to the text of the play newly edited by Professor Halio :

> In his race against time . . . Macbeth emerges as a pattern of absurdity. He is self-defeated. He not only grows old before his time, unable to gain that security he craves, he actually accelerates those forces in and out of time that undermine and finally destroy him. Though he glimpses this absurdity, he perseveres in his course.

It was in this spirit that Hitler states absurdly that it doesn't make any difference whether the Germans fight on the Rhine or elsewhere. They will in any case fight on until 'as Frederick the Great said, one of our damned enemies gets tired'. It was of course Frederick who maintained that experience was only of any value if the right conclusion was drawn from it. In this spirit the Prussian King did at least learn by his mistakes. At Molwitz for example when he first commanded a large body of troops in the field he showed none of that skill for which he was later to be renowned :

> What connoisseurs say of some pictures painted by Raphael in his youth, may be said of this campaign. It was in Frederick's early bad manner. Fortunately for him, the generals to whom he was opposed were men of small capacity. The discipline of his own troops, particularly of the infantry, was unequalled in that age; and some able and experienced officers were at hand to assist him with their advice. . . . Not only, however, did he not establish his title for the

character of an able general; but he was so unfortunate as to make it doubtful whether he possessed the vulgar courage of a soldier. The Cavalry, which he commanded in person, was put to flight. Unaccustomed to the tumult and carnage of a field of battle, he lost his self-possession, and listened too readily to those who urged him to save himself. His English grey carried him many miles from the field. . . . He was successful; but he owed his success to dispositions which others had made, and to the valour of men who had fought while he was flying. So unpromising was the first appearance of the greatest warrior of that age.

How different was the début of the greatest strategic genius of all time as a commander of large armies, and yet how like his great hero, Frederick, Hitler was in other respects. In their approach to war and their strategic aims, they had one supremely important motive in common. Their desire for and determination to have war were equally strong. They were both resolved to embark on a quest for power, the domination of Europe, a *Griff nach der Weltmacht*. Anything would serve for an excuse. Frederick did not pretend to believe idle tales about Prussia's claim to Silesia. 'Ambition, interest, the desire of making people talk about me,' he wrote, 'carried the day; and I decided for war.' Hitler's prefabricated justifications for making impossible demands on Poland were essentially the same. You simply went on making territorial claims until someone said No. Then you attacked them with overwhelming strength and immediate success. Political pressures were to be kept hand in hand with military gains. It was all absurdly simple, and it worked as long as the military gains continued. But once cut off that source of negotiating strength, once set a scene of adversity and then a new line was necessary.

Frederick showed his real greatness in adversity. Hitler showed his absolute evil and nihilism in adversity. An inexorable refusal to spare themselves, a reluctance to compromise, a granite hardness, an infinite inflexibility – these qualities the two men shared. Both loved to dictate, interfere, to savour their power, and make others feel it, both were incapable either of harbouring or inspiring affection, both brought a malice, a love of humiliating others, pettiness, sly cynicism to their everyday handling of affairs. But whatever his other failings, Frederick did not delude himself. The facts might be unpalatable, but he did at least recognize them for what they were, and did not put himself into the trick, as so many other military leaders have done, of closing his eyes to the truth and substituting for it his own wishes and imagination.

M

It was in precisely this fatal luxury that Hitler indulged himself to the full. No deduction, no opinion, no technical or tactical estimate, no judgment which ran contrary to his own was allowed to influence the handling of military situations. Such obstinacy was all very well at a time when Hitler made a habit of being intuitively right and was batting on a good strategic wicket, when the Wehrmacht was opposed to armies less well equipped, led and spirited than it was itself. But turn the tables on the Wehrmacht, put it in a position where – leaving spirit aside – its enemies' leaders and weapons were at least the equal of its own, add a wholly unfavourable tactical situation, give its opponents almost unchallenged command of the air, and then such obstinacy could only compound the difficulties and hasten defeat. Frederick had at the end of the Seven Years War, as Macaulay put it, 'given an example unrivalled in history of what capacity and resolution can effect against the greatest superiority of power and the utmost spite of fortune.' But unharness capacity from this peerless combination, put in its place utter and total incapacity, and resolution alone can do little.

So that in their actual conduct of operations their essential difference was this. Frederick while undismayed by formidable odds, remained an empiricist. Hitler, equally undismayed by equally formidable odds, refused to recognize any condition but his own will. Likenesses remain mixed with contrasts. The vulgar courage of a soldier Hitler had amply displayed during the First World War. Nor as Führer was he a stranger to the intricacies of policy. Just as Frederick in getting his grip on Silesia first betrayed his undertaking to Austria, and then later betrayed his allies in arms against Austria, so Hitler first betrayed Poland and then betrayed his ally in arms against Poland. The great difference between the two men as military leaders – leaving aside those of bent, character, temperament, intellect, accomplishment and inclination – was in their treatment of military experience. Frederick could hardly be said to have distinguished himself on the battlefield of Molwitz – unless it be for lack of steadiness and loss of control. But he did not allow it to discourage him – just as he did not allow the battle of Chotusitz (whose successful conclusion was the result not of his own military skill, although he displayed both vigour and personal bravery there, but of the training, constancy and performance of his troops) to dissuade him that he was still a learner.

The memorable year 1745 followed – memorable in the life of Frederick as the date at which his noviciate in the art of war may be said to have terminated. There have been great captains whose precocious and self-taught military skill resembled intuition. Condé, Clive and Napoleon are examples. But Frederick was not one of these brilliant portents. His proficiency in military science was simply the proficiency which a man of vigorous faculties makes in any science to which he applies his mind with earnestness and industry. It was at Hohenfriedberg that he first proved how much he had profited by his errors, and by their consequences. His victory on that day was chiefly due to his skilful dispositions and convinced Europe that the Prince who, a few years before, had stood aghast in the rout of Molwitz, had attained in the military art a mastery equalled by none of his contemporaries, or equalled by Saxe alone.

If Frederick profited by his errors, Hitler failed to profit by his successes. He was in the early stages of the war and in the years immediately preceding the war so devastatingly and speedily successful – very often in the teeth of his military experts' advice – that he was already too old to learn.

When Berlin was threatened Frederick simply evacuated the city, allowed it to be seized by his enemies, raised yet one more army, and for years gave the most remarkable display of how iron determination, ceaseless activity and sheer competence could stop the rot. To turn the scales of overwhelming enemy superiority, however, he needed more and got more. The death of the Czarina Elizabeth was simply a colossal stroke of luck. Then followed an absolute somersaulting of his fortunes which enabled him to ride in triumph through the streets of his capital. When Frederick's Berlin was threatened in 1759 he put up a fight, and what a fight! His enemies took more than a year to occupy it – but he let it go when capitulation was inevitable. It did not decide the outcome of the war. He merely carried on the struggle elsewhere. In 1760 Berlin was taken by Russian and Austrian troops. Yet Frederick's triumphal re-entry into the city – or what was left of it – was not prevented by its fall. When some two hundred years later Berlin was again threatened, Hitler followed the example of his great hero in only one respect. He refused to admit defeat. But as for activity – apart from the questionable activity of futile military conferences, orders unrelated to military facts and a good deal of bellowing and blood-letting – there was none that made any difference. And as for competence, there was none at all.

After a life of almost unimaginable and ceaseless activity, Napoleon retired to St Helena. There he spent an almost unimaginably long six years of inactivity. But he did what both generals and historians often do. He produced his version of events. It is a tribute to Napoleon's reputation that even his own memoirs could do little to tarnish it. If Hitler, like Napoleon, had written his memoirs, what a version – or perversion – of events that would have been! They could not in any case have further blackened his reputation, for nothing could do that. They would simply have reinforced Burckhardt's contention that all versions of military events must 'wither in time into mere recognition by specialists and military historians'.

BIBLIOGRAPHY

Berlin, Sir Isaiah, *Mr Churchill in 1940*, London, 1949
Bialer, Seweryn, Ed., *Stalin and his Generals*, London, 1949
Bullock, Alan, *Hitler, A Study in Tyranny*, Revised Edition, London, 1962

Chuikov, Vasili I., *The End of the Third Reich*, London, 1967
Churchill, Winston S., *The Second World War*, London, 1949–1954
Clark, Alan, *Barbarossa*, London, 1965
Cookridge, E. H., *Gehlen Spy of the Century*, London, 1971

Donnison, F. S. V., *Civil Affairs and Military Government, North-West Europe* London, 1961

Ehrman, John, *Grand Strategy* (Vol VI), London, 1956
Eisenhower, Dwight D., *Crusade in Europe*, London, 1949
Ellis, Major L. F., *Victory in the West, Vol II*, London, 1968
Essame, H., *The Battle for Germany*, London, 1969

Flannery, H. W., *Assignment to Berlin*, New York, 1942
Fredborg, A., *Behind the Steel Wall*, a Swedish Journalist in Berlin, New York, 1944

de Gaulle, Gen. Charles, *War Memoirs*, Vol II Unity 1942–1944, London, 1959
Gilbert, Felix, Ed., *Hitler Directs his War*, Oxford, 1950
Guderian, Gen. Heinz, *Panzer Leader*, London, 1952

Hechler, Ken, *The Bridge at Remagen,* New York, 1957

Hitler Adolf, *Mein Kampf,* London, 1939; *The Speeches of Adolf Hitler, 1922–39* Ed., Norman H Baynes, 2 vols, Oxford, 1942; *Hitler's Table Talk, 1941–44,* London, 1953; *The Testament of Adolf Hitler: The Hitler-Bormann Documents, February-April 1945,* London, 1961; *Hitler's War Directives 1939–1945,* Ed., H R Trevor-Roper, London, 1964

Kardorff, U. von, *Diary of a Nightmare, Berlin 1942–45,* London 1965

Keitel, Field-Marshal Wilhelm, *The Memoirs of Field-Marshal Keitel,* London, 1965

Kuby, E., *The Russians and Berlin, 1945,* London, 1965

Liddell Hart, Captain Sir Basil, *The Tanks,* 2 vols, London, 1959

McKee, Alexander, *The Race for the Rhine Bridges,* London, 1971

Preston, Chaney Otto, Jr., *Zhukov,* Oklahoma, 1971

Rauschning, Hermann, *Hitler Speaks,* London, 1939

Roskill, S. W., *The War at Sea,* Vol III, Part II, London, 1961

Ryan, C., *The Last Battle,* London, 1966

Schramm, Percy Ernst, *Hitler, The Man and the Military Leader,* London, 1972

Seaton, Albert, *The Russo-German War 1941–45,* London, 1971

Simonov, Konstantin, *Aus den Kriegstagebüchern,* Moscow, 1965

Smith, H. K., *Last Train from Berlin,* London, 1942

Smith, R. Brett-, *Berlin '45; the grey city,* London, 1966

Speer, Albert, *Erinnerungen,* Berlin, 1969

Studnitz, H. G. von, *While Berlin Burns,* London, 1964

Toland, John, *The Last 100 Days,* London, 1966

Trevor-Roper, H. R., *The Last Days of Hitler,* London, 1947; Ed., *Hitler's War Directives 1939–45,* London, 1964

Troyanovsky, Lt Col. P., *The Last Days of Berlin,* Soviet News, 1945

Tully, A., *Berlin, the story of a battle,* New York, 1963

Warlimont, Gen. Walter, *Inside Hitler's Headquarters 1939–1945,* London, 1964

Webster, Sir Charles, and Noble Frankland, *The Strategic Air Offensive against Germany 1939–1945*, Vol III, London, 1961

Weidling, Gen. Helmuth., *Der Endkampf in Berlin*, Potsdam, 1962

Wenck, Gen. W., *Berlin's Last 100 Days*, 1965

Wheeler-Bennett, Sir John and Anthony Nicholls, *The Semblance of Peace*, London, 1972

Wilmot, Chester, *The Struggle for Europe*, London, 1952

Woodward, Sir Llewellyn, *British Foreign Policy in the Second World War*, London, 1962

Zhukov, Georgi K., *Marshal Zhukov's Greatest Battles*, London, 1969

Ziemke, E. F., *The Battle for Berlin; End of the Third Reich*, London, 1969

Ziemke, E. F., *The Soviet's Lost Opportuninty; Berlin in February, 1945*, London, 1969

INDEX